PENGUIN BOOKS

SECRET DOSSIER

Pierre Salinger began his news career at the *San Francisco Chronicle*. From 1961 to 1963 he served as press secretary to President John F. Kennedy and, at the request of President Lyndon B. Johnson, remained in that position until March 1964. He was elected to the United States Senate in August 1964. After joining ABC News as a contributing correspondent in Paris in 1977, he became a full-time correspondent in 1978. A year later, he was appointed ABC News Paris Bureau chief and became its chief foreign correspondent in 1983. He has covered an enormous range of international stories for ABC News. *America Held Hostage: The Secret Negotiations,* a three-hour exclusive report on America's behind-the-scenes efforts to free the American hostages in Iran, won all of America's top TV-journalism prizes, as did his investigation into the bombing of Pan Am 103 over Lockerbie, Scotland. In 1978 the French government decorated him with the Chevalier de la Légion d'honneur and in 1988 he was promoted to Officier de la Legion d'honneur.

Eric Laurent studied the science of communications at the University of Berkeley in California. In 1973 he joined Radio-France as a journalist and from 1978 to 1981 was assistant to Jean-Jacques Servan Schreiber. He then worked as chief reporter for Radio-France, specializing in foreign affairs from 1985 until 1990. He is the author of many books, including *Pétrole à l'heure arabe* (1974), *Vodka-Cola* (1977), *La puce et les géants* (1983), *La corde pour les pendre* (1985), and a novel, *Karl Marx Avenue* (1987), which has been translated into four languages. He now works for *Le Figaro* magazine.

SECRET DOSSIER

THE HIDDEN AGENDA BEHIND THE GULF WAR

PIERRE SALINGER
ERIC LAURENT

Translated from the French
by Howard Curtis

PENGUIN BOOKS

PENGUIN BOOKS

Published by the Penguin Group
Viking Penguin, a division of Penguin Books USA Inc.,
375 Hudson Street, New York, New York 10014, U.S.A.
Penguin Books Ltd, 27 Wrights Lane,
London W8 5TZ, England
Penguin Books Australia Ltd, Ringwood,
Victoria, Australia
Penguin Books Canada Ltd, 2801 John Street,
Markham, Ontario, Canada L3R 1B4
Penguin Books (N.Z.) Ltd, 182–190 Wairau Road,
Auckland 10, New Zealand

Penguin Books Ltd, Registered Offices:
Harmondsworth, Middlesex, England

First published in France under the title, *Guerre du Golfe: Le Dossier Secret,* by
Olivier Orban 1991. This English translation published by Penguin Books 1991

1 3 5 7 9 10 8 6 4 2

French edition copyright © Olivier Orban, 1991
This English edition copyright © Pierre Salinger and Eric Laurent, 1991
Translation copyright © Howard Curtis, 1991

Printed in the United States of America
Set in Times Roman

CONTENTS

v

PREFACE

When Saddam Hussein invaded Kuwait on August 2, 1990, I was starting my quiet annual vacation on Nantucket Island, off the coast of Massachusetts. The New York foreign news desk of ABC News called me late on the evening of August 1 to tell me what had happened. Even though the vacation lasted another two weeks, I was immediately involved in getting in touch with my Middle East sources and providing information for a number of ABC news shows. Some of the information gathered in the first few days turned out to be perfectly true—that Saddam Hussein would use Western hostages as human shields at key military locations; that, if a war broke out, he would launch Scud missiles against Saudi Arabia and Israel; and that King Hussein of Jordan and the leader of the PLO, Yasser Arafat, were involved in back-channel negotiations to try to solve the crisis rapidly. I returned to London, then headed for the Middle East and, over a period of several months, visited Jordan, Iraq, Syria, and Tunisia. I was also in touch with sources in Egypt, Saudi Arabia, and Kuwait.

My contacts, often at the highest possible level in these countries, led me to discover two important scenarios that make up this book—what happened between the end of the Iran–Iraq war on August 8, 1988, and the invasion of Kuwait on August 2, 1990, that stimulated Saddam Hussein to make this invasion, and how the Arab world tried desperately to solve the problem quickly, particularly through King Hussein of Jordan, only to find its efforts undercut by pressure from the United States government, pushing Arab nations to join its condemnation of Saddam Hussein's invasion of Kuwait. This is not a book about war. It is a book that shows how war could have been avoided. As we went through the crisis, it became clear that few nations in the anti-Iraq alliance could tolerate the dictatorship and brutality of Saddam Hussein and therefore were not really interested in a peaceful solution that would have left him in power, heavily armed. But this book also shows that a strongly armed Saddam Hussein was entirely the responsibility of Western nations and the Soviet Union, which ended up in the anti-Iraq coalition. It is also clear that at the start of 1990 the United States was sending mixed messages to Iraq, convincing it that military action against Kuwait would not provoke American retaliation. The Americans did not understand Saddam Hussein or his mentality, and Saddam Hussein did not understand the United States and its mentality. Saddam Hussein did not understand the improvement of relations between the United States and the Soviet Union either. When he invaded Kuwait, he was convinced that, if the United States intervened against him, he would have the Soviet Union as an ally. For a long time he did not believe President Bush's threats that the American-led coalition would not tolerate his decision to stay in Kuwait. The result was war.

SECRET DOSSIER

1

"I Shall Retaliate"

On August 8, 1988, the Iran–Iraq war came to an end. Little did anyone suspect that this date would also mark the beginning of the Gulf crisis of 1990–91.

If only because Tehran had been the first to propose a cease-fire, Iraq was seen as the victor of a conflict that, in eight years, had cost nearly 1 million lives. In point of fact, the end of the war left Iraq both powerful and drained of resources. Its military machine was more impressive than that of any other country in the region: 55 divisions, as against 10 divisions in 1980; 1 million men, all highly trained and ready to fight; 500 planes; and 5,500 tanks. But the scale of the financial disaster was just as enormous. At the beginning of the war Iraq had held reserves of $30 billion. Eight years later it was in debt to the tune of nearly $100 billion. Saddam Hussein never lost an opportunity to tell the foreign guests he welcomed to his presidential palace—a cold, imposing building in the heart of Baghdad—that for those eight years he had been like "a shield protecting my Arab brothers from the Persian threat" and that he expected

1

"the richest of them, Saudi Arabia, the United Arab Emirates and Kuwait, to help us to pay off all our debts."

On August 9, 1988, just one day after Iran accepted the cease-fire, Kuwait took the decision to increase its oil production, in violation of the agreements signed within the Organization of Petroleum Exporting Countries (OPEC). In particular, it intended to extract more from the wells at Rumailah, which is situated in a border region long claimed by Iraq and the subject of bitter diplomatic debate.

For Saddam Hussein the Kuwaiti move was an act of betrayal and provocation. It would make the present situation of over-production and falling prices even worse. Iraq's revenues, which were 90 percent dependent on oil, would fall to $7 billion a year, while the cost of servicing the country's debt would rise to $7 billion. Iraq would be slowly strangled.

It would be hard to imagine two countries more dissimilar than Iraq and Kuwait. In Iraq all the power was in the hands of one man, a ruthless dictator obsessed with power and the rule of force. By comparison with this country of 18 million people, characterized by austerity and hardship, the Emirate of Kuwait was a tiny enclave of wealth and plenty, where the thousand members of the reigning Al Sabah family divided up all the important jobs, all the positions of influence and all the profits among themselves, as might a board of directors. Kuwaiti investments abroad were in excess of $100 billion and each year brought in an income of $6 billion—that is, more than the revenues from oil. It was a bonanza that benefited, above all, the 700,000 people who had Kuwaiti citizenship; the 1,200,000 migrant workers who made the wheels of the economy go round—Palestinians, Filipinos, Pakistanis, Egyptians—were left with the crumbs from the rich man's table.

Money often renders people arrogant and blind. The leaders of Kuwait were no exception. Their arrogance and blindness made the ensuing drama almost inevitable—a drama of which nobody had read the warning signs and which erupted in a tragic war.

Late in the morning of February 12, 1990—Abraham Lincoln's birthday—John Kelly arrived in Baghdad. He was in his late forties, of medium height, with brown hair, calm in appearance and restrained in his gestures. A career diplomat who had specialized in European affairs and had previously held only one post in the Middle East, an Ambassador to Lebanon, Kelly was paying his first official visit to Iraq as Assistant Secretary of State with responsibility for the Middle East. It was a cold day, and the U.S. Ambassador in Baghdad, April Glaspie, was waiting for him on the tarmac, in the company of two Iraqi officials. April Glaspie, a sharp-faced, austere-looking woman, had embarked on a diplomatic career after graduating from Johns Hopkins University. She spoke fluent Arabic and had held several posts, notably in Tunis and Damascus, before becoming head of the bureau responsible for monitoring Jordanian, Lebanese and Syrian affairs at the State Department. She was unmarried and lived in Baghdad with her mother and her dog. Since her arrival she had not been granted a single private interview with Saddam Hussein.

The reports on the Iraqi President that the State Department had drawn up had explored three main points: his desire and ability to become the true leader of the Arab world; his fascination with the prestige and charisma of Egypt's former leader Gamal Abdel Nasser, with whom he liked to identify; and, finally, his rapprochement with the West. John Kelly and his advisers considered this last point to be the most significant. When Iraqi troops had attacked Iran in 1980 the Ba'athist regime had been classed as one of Moscow's strongest allies in the region. In 1978, after the signing of the Camp David agree-

3

ment between Israel and Egypt, Baghdad had even headed the rejection front that was formed with the object of isolating and punishing Cairo for its rapprochement with the Jewish state. At that time Iraq had also provided shelter for the most violent Palestinian terrorist groups, notably that of Abu Nidal.

Eight years later Iraq emerged from the war closer to the West than it had ever been. Its economy was more closely linked with Western countries than with the Soviet Union, and its military arsenal was made up of material acquired as much from Western Europe, especially France, as from Moscow. All this led the Americans to stake their money on Iraq as a powerful force for stability in the region.

John Kelly was received by Saddam Hussein on the afternoon of February 12, 1990. This was the President's first interview with an American official for a long time. In the course of their cordial exchanges John Kelly told his host: "You are a force for moderation in the region, and the United States wishes to broaden her relations with Iraq."

Saddam Hussein was extremely flattered—indeed "proud," to use his own word—to hear these remarks, and in the hours that followed the interview he quoted them to several Arab heads of state. The first person he telephoned was King Hussein of Jordan.

What John Kelly had formulated was the first of a whole series of ambiguous and contradictory messages that were to be fraught with serious consequences.

On February 15, three days after this interview, the Voice of America, in its broadcasts to the Arab world, transmitted a program that "reflected," according to its presenter, "the views of the American government." It was an appeal to public opinion to mobilize against the dictators who still held sway around the world. Iraq was one of the countries mentioned, and Saddam Hussein was condemned as one of the worst tyrants in the world. The Iraqi President flew into a violent rage, and although Washington sent him an apology via its Baghdad embassy, he refused to accept that the Voice of America could express an opinion that differed from the official view. Coming so soon after the praise he had received from John Kelly, this incident seemed to prove to Hussein that the Americans were playing a double game. And as if to confirm him in this impression, on February 21 the State Department published a report on human rights that included twelve pages on Iraq. Saddam Hussein's government was described as "the worst violator of human rights." The frequent use of torture and numerous summary executions were both mentioned. No sooner had this report been published than the Foreign Affairs Committee of the House of Representatives proposed the adoption of a resolution condemning Iraq for its "gross violations of human rights." The Bush administration protested vigorously against this move and blocked its adoption.

All these contradictory signals revealed that the American leadership was not concentrating seriously on what was happening in the Middle East. Neither Iraq nor the Middle East was seen as a current priority. All of President Bush's attention and energy, and those of his closest colleagues—especially Secretary of State James Baker—were focused on the dialogue with the Soviet Union and the remarkable explosion of democracy in Eastern Europe. The world media were also looking in the wrong direction and would completely fail to pick up the signals coming out of the Middle East. A dramatic example occurred in late February.

On February 23, 1990, Saddam Hussein arrived in Jordan's capital, Amman. The flight plan of his plane and its time of arrival had been kept secret until the last moment. Fearing an assassination attempt, the Iraqi President had traveled in an unmarked jet, while the plane he usually used for official jour-

PIERRE SALINGER WITH ERIC LAURENT

neys had landed a few hours earlier with his colleagues and his bodyguards on board. Greeted on the tarmac by King Hussein, the President seemed tense and worried. He was in Amman to take part in the ceremonies to mark the first anniversary of the Arab Cooperation Council (ACC), a regional club that the King of Jordan considered of great importance but did not seem of particular interest to Saddam Hussein. The ACC was made up of Iraq, Egypt, Yemen, and Jordan. The occasion did not, in fact, attract very much attention either among the Arab public or among the few Western journalists who were present in Amman. Nobody could have foreseen what was to be said, especially behind the scenes. Saddam Hussein treated an audience of his peers to a fierce speech in which he predicted that the weakening of the power of Moscow would give the United States unprecedented freedom of action in the Middle East over the next five years. "Isn't Washington helping Soviet Jews to emigrate to Israel? Aren't American ships still patrolling the Gulf, even though the war between Iran and Iraq is over?" For Saddam Hussein, whose speech was broadcast on Jordanian television, the reasons for America's behavior were obvious: "The country that exerts the greatest influence on the region, on the Gulf and its oil, will consolidate its superiority as an unrivaled superpower. This proves that if the population of the Gulf—and of the entire Arab world—is not vigilant, this area will be ruled according to the wishes of the United States. For example, the price of oil will be fixed for the benefit of American interests, and everyone else's interests will be ignored." Saddam's messsage to his peers was clear: the interests of the Arab world were best served by Iraq's, not the United States', domination of the Gulf.

This statement angered Egypt's President Hosni Mubarak, America's main ally in the region. Every year Cairo received more than $2 billion in aid from Washington. Saddam Hussein had also suggested in his speech that oil money invested in the West should be withdrawn in order to shift American policy. "There is no place among good Arabs," he added, "for cowards who claim that a superpower, the United States, should decide everything and that everyone else should submit." Mubarak took these words as a personal attack. He left the room in a rage, and all his delegation followed him. To a worried King Hussein, who went after him, Mubarak said, "Those remarks are intolerable. I'm going back to Egypt."

The King tried to smooth things over by proposing a meeting with the Iraqi President to clear up the misunderstanding. Mubarak flatly refused at first but finally yielded to persuasion. The three men met on the evening of February 24 in the Hashemiel Palace, where Hussein had lived before his previous wife, Queen Alia, died in a helicopter crash. The atmosphere was tense. Instead of being conciliatory, Saddam Hussein was even more exigent. Speaking dryly, his eyes never wandering from the other two men, he recalled the $30 billion he had been loaned by Kuwait and Saudi Arabia during the war against Iran. "If they don't cancel the debt and give me another $30 billion, I shall take steps to retaliate."

Exasperated beyond measure, Mubarak replied angrily: "Your demands don't make any sense. You're going to cause a lot of trouble." He cut short the meeting and returned to Cairo that night. King Hussein was forced to cancel the second day of ACC debates.

The furor surrounding Saddam Hussein's speech and the extent of his demands sent ripples of anxiety around the Arab world. In particular, the leaders of Kuwait and Saudi Arabia feared that Baghdad would either use its missiles to launch a surprise attack against them, followed by invasion, or instigate a series of terrorist acts, with members of the two royal families as targets.

7

In Riyadh Saudi officials quickly alerted the local Central Intelligence Agency (CIA) station to the threat hanging over them. The information was passed on to CIA headquarters in Langley, near Washington, but there was no reaction from the Bush administration. The CIA nevertheless decided to place Iraq "under surveillance" and to increase its intelligence-gathering activities in the country. The main problem was the lack of access to reliable sources. The wheels of power in Baghdad were controlled entirely by Saddam Hussein and members of his family, supported by an efficient and omnipresent secret police force. William Casey, director of the CIA under Reagan, had been forced to admit that the Agency did not have a single skilled agent in Iraq, and the situation had not changed since.

Meanwhile a confidential report on the state of the Iraqi economy, written in late February by one of the most influential bankers in the Middle East, had been circulating in the principal Arab capitals. The report began by recalling that between 1972 and 1980, the year in which the war against Iran had started, the annual oil revenue of Iraq had increased from $1 billion to $25 billion. But at the beginning of 1990 the outlook for the country was grim. Deploying a mixture of hard facts and metaphor, the banker stated: "The brilliant kaleidoscope of the seventies is in marked contrast to the current dismal reality of the economy, the vast amount of destruction all over the country and the total lack of hope for future generations. Can anything be done about this depressing state of affairs? Sadly, I have to report that, under the present government, the situation can only get worse." He stressed that the huge accumulated debt, on which Baghdad could not even pay the interest, "would lead to a dangerous and foolhardy policy of further borrowing, at rates of 30 percent per annum." He also revealed the surprising fact that in 1989 Iraq had been the biggest user in the world of the American Community Credit Program, designed to sell U.S. agricultural produce abroad.

The most interesting paragraph of the report was the last one. With remarkable foresight it predicted what would, in fact, happen: "Saddam Hussein is now perfectly aware of his financial situation. What are the options open to him in Iraq herself? There are very few. But there is always Kuwait, situated just a few miles from where his idle army is massed on the Shatt-al-Arab. Iraq needs to gain access to the open waters of the Gulf."

There were clues to the increasing difficulties facing Baghdad in the many ambitious projects that had been curtailed, such as the building of a subway system in the capital, the laying of more than 1,800 miles of railway track, and the construction of two huge hydroelectric dams.

Another observer of the growing dissension within the "family of Arabs"—a family to which Saddam Hussein referred constantly both in his speeches and in private conversations with a few trusted friends—was King Hussein of Jordan. Having reigned for an astonishing thirty-seven years—a reign characterized both by an awareness of its own fragility and by an astonishing instinct for survival—the King was more sensitive than anyone to the signals that warned of impending crises. He knew that a further political upheaval in the region could endanger his country's very existence. With a population of 3 million—60 percent of them Palestinian—and a total lack of resources, Jordan could easily be wiped off the map. "I can feel the tension mounting," he told a visitor, speaking in a solemn and dispassionate tone, "just as it did before the 1967 war. I've been in power for nearly forty years, and I've never known the region to be at such a dangerous crossroads as it is now." On the wall just behind him hung a photograph of Saddam Hussein.

The Iraqi President was an ally but also a source of concern, a powerful partner without whom Jordan, in her weakness, could not manage but also a leader whose openly expressed ambitions could destabilize the precarious balance of power in the region. After the failure of the meeting in Amman on February 24, King Hussein had suggested to the Iraqi President that he, the King, should visit the Gulf states to try to reach an agreement between Kuwait, Saudi Arabia, and Iraq. He set off on February 26 and for three days flew from one capital to another, holding detailed discussions with all the leaders of the region. He returned to Amman, exhausted, on the night of March 1.

On the morning of March 3 Saddam Hussein telephoned him: "A plane's on its way. I'm expecting you in Baghdad."

The two men met for more than four hours, during which King Hussein gave a blow-by-blow account of his journey.

One thing was clear: negotiations seemed impossible. The leaders of the Gulf states had not given the King a single positive sign. Saddam Hussein had three objectives: to settle his border disputes with Kuwait, in particular the problem of the high-yielding Rumailah oil fields situated in the disputed area; to rent two islands, Warba and Bubiyan, from the Emirate, thus giving Iraq a vital access to the Gulf; and, finally, to solve the problem of the debt accumulated during the war with Iran.

King Hussein told him that the Emir of Kuwait refused to enter into any negotiations until Iraq officially recognized Kuwaiti sovereignty. The Baghdad government had, in fact, recognized the independence of Kuwait in 1963, but the Revolution Command Council, which effectively controlled the country, had overturned the decision soon afterward.

Comfortably settled in a big armchair, his eyes half-closed, occasionally lighting a cigarette, Saddam Hussein listened carefully to the King's words. He did not lose his temper. It was as if he had anticipated that the results of the King's trip would be negative. He thanked his guest profusely for his efforts at mediation and told him that he hoped that "in time, reason and goodwill would finally prevail in this matter." These were unusually restrained and conciliatory words from a man who had accustomed his colleagues to dread his fits of rage. (Hosni Mubarak, who never hid his deep antipathy toward the Iraqi President, summed up the feelings of several Arab leaders when he called Saddam Hussein "a real psychopath.")

A mere three days after the King had returned to Amman Saddam Hussein summoned all the members of his military high command to a secret meeting and told them to immediately draw up plans for the massing of troops on the border with Kuwait.

Although nothing had yet happened, the tension was mounting rapidly. During this period the Kuwaitis showed a foresight that they were tragically to lack a few months later. Two weeks after the order to the Iraqi high command to prepare for the deployment of troops in the border area a highly placed Kuwaiti official passed through Amman. Not a single Iraqi division had yet moved, yet the official told the Jordanians in confidence that "Saddam Hussein doesn't want just those two islands that would give him access to the Gulf; he wants the whole of Kuwait."

2

A Violent History

For more than a century London had regarded the Gulf virtually as British territory, giving it control over the route to India and the Far East. London's clear determination to allow no one else to exercise influence over the region, together with the tactical shrewdness of its diplomats, helped to plant the seeds of the present conflict.

Until the First World War Iraq and Kuwait had both been part of the Ottoman Empire. In fact, Kuwait, with its tiny land surface of just over 10,000 square miles, had been part of the Iraqi *vilayat* (administrative district) of Basra. In 1913, while the rumblings of war were growing louder in Europe, the British and the Turks had signed an agreement making Kuwait an autonomous district. In the middle of the war, with the Turks fighting on the side of the Germans, London recognized the Emirate and its borders as totally independent of the Ottoman Empire.

This partition, which gave the British an important strategic ally, was never accepted by the Iraqis, who felt frustrated at being denied access to the Gulf and at losing an area of land that, as far as they were concerned, had never had an independent existence.

Iraq, which became a British mandate in 1918, had another cause for resentment. In 1925 the government in Baghdad was forced to sign an agreement with a giant oil consortium, the Iraq Petroleum Company (IPC). The agreement stipulated, in particular, that the company should remain in British hands, that its managing director should be a British subject, and that the concession should remain in force until the year 2000. The IPC had *carte blanche* to exploit the most fantastic petroleum deposits in the history of the oil industry as it saw fit and to make colossal profits.

In point of fact, in a region where the borders were very imprecise Iraq was just as much of an artificial creation as Kuwait. Following the Sykes–Picot agreement of 1916, which divided the spoils of the Ottoman Empire between Britain and France, Iraq had been formed out of three former Turkish provinces: Baghdad, Basra and Mosul. This state of affairs has been summed up brilliantly in one sentence: "Iraq was created by Churchill, who had the mad idea of joining two widely separated oil wells, Kirkuk and Mosul, by uniting three widely separated peoples: the Kurds, the Sunnis and the Shi'ites."

Perhaps because of this difficult and uncertain birth, modern Iraq has had a consistently violent history. In 1958 the pro-Western monarchy was overthrown, King Faisal was murdered, and his Prime Minister, Noury Said, was stoned to death by a mob. Two years later the new leader, General Kassem, narrowly escaped an assassination attempt. Among the would-be assassins was a twenty-two-year-old named Saddam Hussein who, although wounded, managed to escape to Syria.

In 1963 Kassem's head was paraded through the streets on

a pike by an angry mob. In 1968 the Ba'ath Party came to power. This was Saddam Hussein's triumph. He was then only vice-president of the Revolution Command Council, but he was already the most powerful man in the country. The security services were then, and still are, controlled by his three half-brothers, Barzan, Sabawi, and Wathban; his cousin, Ali Hassam Al Majid, was to be responsible for the virtual genocide of the Kurds, accomplished largely through the use of chemical weapons against civilians. Hussein Kamal Al-Majid, Saddam's son-in-law, was the key figure in the procurement of military material, earning a substantial commission on each contract. He is said to have made $60 million from the purchase of 120 Chinese-made Scud missiles in 1987.

This small group in power in Baghdad is linked by ties of blood—especially other people's blood. Saddam's eldest son, Uday, had one of his father's bodyguards beaten to death in front of guests. In a rage, Saddam threatened to kill his son. His first wife, Sajida, asked her brother, Adnan Khayrallah, who was also Minister of Defense, to intercede on Uday's behalf. Saddam spared his son but never forgave his minister, although he was his brother-in-law and his cousin. Saddam ordered his execution, and his death was disguised as a helicopter crash. Violence is Saddam Hussein's main weapon. When he attained supreme power in 1979 he celebrated the occasion by ordering the execution of twenty-one members of his cabinet, including one of his closest friends, for whom he had this epitaph: "He was very close to me, but he grew too distant."

A year later he summoned several of his ministers and colleagues to the main prison in Baghdad to serve as a firing squad. The victims were political prisoners. It was his way of offering a foretaste of what might happen to anyone who might be tempted to oppose his will. He summed up this episode with consummate cynicism by saying: "The most loyal are those who've been found guilty."

As someone who has never been a soldier, Saddam is fascinated with the army and at the same time mistrusts it. He wants it to be powerful and yet pliable. He may like to appear dressed in a general's uniform, but he still has an inferiority complex toward his commanding officers, most of whom consider him an upstart. This is the reason for his mass purges. During the Iran–Iraq war it was rumored that many high-ranking military men had been shot. Saddam put the record straight: "Only two divisional commanders and the head of a mechanized unit have been executed. That's quite normal in a war."

Be that as it may, when an officer rose during a meeting of the high command to argue against Saddam's plan for launching an offensive, the President listened to his criticisms, then, without a word, drew the revolver he always carries on his belt and shot him in the head.

In 1988, shortly after the ending of hostilities, hundreds of officers were sent to prison, and many of them were subsequently killed. Such was the fate of one of the heroes of the war, General Maher Abdul Rashid, whose daughter had been married to one of Saddam's sons.

A report on human rights, published in 1990, stated: "Under the Ba'ath Party, Iraq has become a nation of informers." A sad definition but an accurate one: it has been calculated that almost 25 percent of the population, one Iraqi in four, works for one or another of the security services, which were trained, and for a long time supervised, by specialists from the East German secret police, the STASI.

Saddam Hussein loves to attend frequent private showings of his favorite film: *The Godfather*. He also likes to compare

himself with Nebuchadnezzar, King of Babylon from 605 to 562
B.C., probably because this political ancestor of his, who like
him believed in the rule of force, seized Jerusalem, destroyed
the Temple, and sent the Jewish people into captivity.

Napoleon confessed that he based his plans of battle on the
dreams of his sleeping soldiers. Saddam Hussein's war plans
and dreams of glory are dependent on the generosity and complicity of the Western democracies. In 1984 Iraq spent $14 bil-
lion—half its gross national product—on buying arms. Between
1982 and 1985, it imported some $42.8 billion worth of arma-
ments. These purchases showed no signs of decreasing after the
cease-fire with Iran. In the previous five years Baghdad had
been the biggest importer of military material in the world,
bidding for 10 percent of all the arms sold worldwide.

From having been an ally of Moscow, with which he signed
a "treaty of friendship and cooperation" in 1972, Saddam Hussein had developed ever closer ties with the West over the years,
because only the West could supply him with what he needed.
In the mid-1970s, when he wanted to develop a nuclear industry,
the French supplied him with the plant he required, turning a
blind eye to the dangers of proliferation. Saddam Hussein had
never made any secret of wanting to possess nuclear weapons.
(His dreams received a temporary setback in 1981, when Israeli
planes destroyed his nuclear plant at Osiraq.)

He already possessed a large stock of chemical weapons,
which he had used against Iranian troops and Kurdish villagers.
In this case too Western aid had been vital. Experts have now
compiled a list of more than 300 companies that have contributed, to a greater or lesser extent, toward the Iraqi military
buildup, especially in the field of chemical weapons. The countries most involved were Germany, the United States, Britain,
France, Italy, Switzerland, Austria and Belgium. Although the

United States government has always denied supplying Iraq with arms, many private American firms sold military material to Baghdad through other companies that served as intermediaries.

The operation carried out at London's Heathrow Airport on March 28, 1990, revealed the extent of this trade. That day British Customs seized a number of electronic "Krytrons," which could have been used as detonators for nuclear weapons. The haul was the result of eighteen months of investigation and surveillance, conducted jointly by U.S. Customs and British Intelligence. The incriminating parts had been manufactured by a firm in San Diego, California, which had been approached by middle-men working for Iraq. Intrigued by the approach, the directors of the company had alerted the Customs Service, which had infiltrated one of its men into the group taking part in the negotiations for the sale and transfer of the "Krytrons." The material was shipped to London on a TWA cargo flight and stored in the transit area for two weeks. The Customs officers stepped in just as the shipment was about to be loaded into the baggage hold of an Iraqi Airways plane bound for Baghdad. Five employees of the airline were arrested: two Iraqis, one Lebanese, and two Britons.

Another seizure in San Diego led to the arrest of more Britons working for subsidiaries of British companies. The parts thus confiscated left the authorities somewhat surprised. For a year or two reports had been circulating about Baghdad's ambition to build nuclear weapons. The seizure of the "Krytrons" seemed to justify the experts' worst fears. Could it be that the time when Iraq would have an atomic bomb was closer than anyone had envisaged?

Saddam Hussein reacted to the seizures with a speech against the "anti-Arab forces who were trying to put a stop to Iraq's progress." The Iraqi President was in a difficult position.

In September 1989 a terrible explosion devastated the military complex at El-Alexandria, south of Baghdad, where chemical weapons were manufactured. Despite the total information black-out imposed by the regime, eyewitness accounts and photographs taken by spy satellites revealed the extent of the disaster: more than 700 dead and hundreds of others handicapped for life. In February 1990 a journalist working for the London *Observer* tried to investigate the catastrophe. His name was Farzad Bazoft, and he was an Iranian expatriate who carried a British passport. He was arrested by the Iraqi secret police, the dreaded Mukhabarat, run by Saddam Hussein's half-brother Sabawi. Accused of spying for Israel, he appeared on television and made a public confession that had clearly been obtained by force.

The death sentence pronounced on him provoked a wave of protest, not only in Europe and the United States but also among certain Arab officials. A few days after the sentence the Jordanian Foreign Minister, Marwan Al Qasim, was in Tunis for a meeting of Arab foreign ministers. Taking advantage of a moment in private, he spoke to his Iraqi counterpart, Tariq Aziz. "It would be a terrible mistake if your government killed Bazoft. The press will get hold of the affair, and Iraq's image in the West will be severely damaged." Al Qasim was surprised at the violent way in which Tariq Aziz, whom he had known for many years, reacted. The Iraqi minister's curt, angry reply was: "We have to execute him. If we don't, there'll be a thousand spies in Iraq next week."

Farzad Bazoft was hanged on March 15, 1990. The extent of the condemnation upset Saddam Hussein, who could not understand why the Western countries, which had previously been so tolerant toward him, were suddenly so critical. The Bazoft

18

affair, the seizure at Heathrow Airport, and the various about-turns of the Americans finally convinced him that an international campaign was being mounted against his country. As a simple but canny man, who was also proud and power hungry, he now saw Iraq as a beleaguered fortress capable of defying the world that had made her so powerful.

3

"You're Waging Economic War"

On April 2 Saddam Hussein gave a speech to his army officers that was broadcast in full on radio. Sporting a general's insignia on his khaki uniform, he spoke for more than an hour. Parts of his speech were to astonish the whole world. Referring to the new chemical weapons that had been perfected by Iraqi scientists, he declared, "By God, if the Israelis try anything against us, we'll see to it that half their country is destroyed by fire . . . Whoever threatens us with atomic bombs will be exterminated with chemical weapons."

These words reached John Kelly's desk the same day. The Assistant Secretary of State with responsibility for the Middle East read and reread the dispatches he had received, amazed by the violence of their tone. The man who, less than two months earlier, had lavished praise on the Iraqi leader immediately went to see Dennis Ross, whose office was situated a few floors above his in the State Department building. Ross was in charge of the bureau for political planning but, more

20

important, he was one of Secretary of State James Baker's closest colleagues. Kelly was in favor of an immediate and blunt response designed to stress an American refusal to tolerate such threats. As he alternated between a tough line and a conciliatory position John Kelly was becoming the true Dr. Jekyll and Mr. Hyde of the Iraqi affair.

Ross and Kelly quickly worked out an initial plan for sanctions, then went to James Baker's office on the seventh floor. They had to wait only a few moments in the outer office. The Secretary of State listened carefully to what they had to say. "We must send out an unambiguous signal," they told him, "especially by adopting a certain number of retaliatory measures on the economic front." Baker, who was also very disturbed by the aggressiveness of Saddam Hussein's speech, agreed with this suggestion and with the proposals that the two men put forward, of which three were essential: to refuse Iraq funds from the Export–Import Bank; to cancel the Community Credit Program; and, finally, to take measures to prohibit the Iraqi regime from importing "material with a potential military use."

While experts worked to perfect this plan, George Bush gave his opinion of Saddam's threats on board the presidential Boeing, Air Force One. The words he used were vague, reflecting his bewilderment and the fact that Iraq was clearly not one of his top priorities. "I think these statements are very bad. I'm asking Iraq very strongly to immediately reject the use of chemical weapons. I don't think it'll help the Middle East or Iraq's security; I would even say that it'll have the opposite effect. I suggest that such statements about chemical or biological weapons be forgotten."

On April 9 John Kelly and Dennis Ross were once again in James Baker's office. With them was Robert Kimmitt, Under-

Secretary of State for Political Affairs, another member of the narrow circle of Baker's close colleagues.

Baker had been given President Bush's backing, and after being reexamined in detail the plan for economic sanctions was approved. It was Robert Kimmitt who would have the formidable task of negotiating with the various departments and agencies involved in applying the plan. The determination shown at the meeting was, however, quickly to fade, and the sanctions plan was to remain a nonstarter. The reasons for the failure were the resistance of the federal bureaucracy and the lack of political follow-through.

The first reservations came from the Commerce Department, which suggested that the suspension of funds from the Export–Import Bank would penalize American businessmen. Officials of the same department were also opposed to the cancellation of the Community Credit Program, which would, according to them, inflict hardship on American cereal growers.

The National Security Council, the body within the White House responsible for monitoring questions of foreign policy, supported the idea of sanctions but was opposed to applying them too quickly. Robert Gates, the number-two man on the council and former Deputy Director of the CIA, defended this gradual approach. Soon afterward Robert Kimmitt chaired a meeting in the "Situation Room," the control center for the National Security Council. The meeting was attended by the deputy heads of the main government agencies. There was a show of unanimity throughout the meeting, but nobody was fooled. The plan for sanctions against Iraq lay in tatters.

The only man who might have been able to overcome the reservations and impose his views was James Baker. But the Secretary of State's time and thoughts were wholly absorbed by the impending unification of Germany and his frequent trips to meet his Soviet opposite number, Eduard Shevardnadze, in preparation for the Bush–Gorbachev summit that was due to take place in Malta in May. As one of Baker's closest colleagues put it: "The Iraqi missile hadn't yet been picked up by the radar in Washington."

So Saddam Hussein received no official warning. In fact, a certain number of encouraging signs at that time helped to make the American position even more ambiguous.

On April 12, just ten days after the Iraqi President's violent diatribe, a group of five American senators arrived in Baghdad on an official visit. The delegation was led by a senator from Kansas, Robert Dole, who had failed to defeat George Bush in the important primaries in the race for the presidency and was now leader of the Republican minority in the Senate. Saddam Hussein was thus to address a man whom he considered important and influential and, more significantly, whose views were shared by President Bush.

The meeting took place in Mosul, a city in the north of the country, close to the border with Syria. Saddam Hussein, dressed in an elegant gray suit and a dark tie, received the senators in a small sitting room. He sat on a sofa covered in gray velvet. There was a low glass table in the middle of the room, and his guests sat in armchairs around it. An interpreter began by reading a letter that the senators had brought. It opened by declaring that they had come "because we believe that Iraq has a central role to play in the Middle East." It made clear to the Iraqi leader the senators' "conviction that your desire to equip yourself with chemical and biological weapons, far from strengthening your country's security, exposes it to serious dangers. Such moves also threaten other countries and will cause a great deal of trouble throughout the Middle East. Your recent statements, in which you threatened to use chemical weapons against Israel, have caused a stir around the world, and it would be a good thing for you and for peace in the Middle East if you reconsidered such dangerous projects and such provocative statements and acts."

When the reading of the letter was completed Saddam nodded. He had remained completely impassive throughout. Now he turned to Dole, who was sitting on his right-hand side, and said calmly, "I'm aware that a massive campaign has been launched against us by the United States and Europe."

Dole, a somber, severe man in his sixties, immediately replied, "Such a campaign certainly doesn't come from President Bush. He told us only yesterday that he was quite against it." Robert Dole then recalled that the United States had condemned Israel after the attack on the Iraqi nuclear plant in 1981.

"Yes, you condemned them," Saddam Hussein interrupted, "but there have been numerous reports showing that the United States knew of the operation well in advance."

The Republican senator from Wyoming, Alan Simpson, was next to speak. "There's no problem between you and the American government or the American people. Your only problem is with our press, who are arrogant and hard to please."

Robert Dole then moved on to February's broadcast on the Voice of America attacking the Iraqi regime. He apologized for the program, which had "outraged" Saddam Hussein, and informed the President that the journalist responsible had been dismissed. Dole concluded: "Let me point out to you that twelve hours ago President Bush told me that he and his government were hoping to improve relations with Iraq. I can even assure you that President Bush will oppose sanctions. He could even veto any such decision, unless any provocative act should occur."

Ambassador Glaspie, who was present but had remained

silent, now brought the meeting to an end with these words: "As American Ambassador, I can assure you, Mr. President, that this is indeed the policy of the United States government."

There were some domestic political motives behind the conciliatory statements made at this meeting. The senators who had come to Baghdad all represented important farming states. Dole's state, Kansas, for example, exported large quantities of wheat to Iraq. Commercial interests were a major factor in the American desire for moderation. Every year the United States sold Baghdad almost $1 billion worth of wheat, rice, chicken and corn. Since 1983 these exports had been financed largely by loans guaranteed by the U.S. government to the tune of $5 billion.

A representative from Kansas summed up the situation in one sentence: "We supply the Iraqis with all the food they need at subsidized prices."

Nobody had any real desire to jeopardize such fruitful exchanges. When George Bush received the delegation of senators at the White House on their return from Iraq, he listened carefully to Robert Dole's moderate and optimistic statements. The senator saw Saddam Hussein as "the kind of leader the United States can easily be in a position to influence."

Also present at the meeting was General Brent Scowcroft, head of the National Security Council. Scowcroft had spent many years in the corridors of power. He had first entered the White House during the Nixon era, as Henry Kissinger's deputy. A military man, temperamentally inclined to weigh matters carefully and to keep a level head, he agreed with the position taken by Dole: Iraq and its leader were vital factors in the political balance of the Middle East.

On April 25, as an indication of this new-found peace of mind, George Bush sent a message of friendship to Saddam

PIERRE SALINGER WITH ERIC LAURENT

Hussein to mark the end of Ramadan. In it he expressed the hope that "the ties between the United States and Iraq would contribute to the peace and stability of the Middle East."

Not long afterward John Kelly testified before the Senate Foreign Affairs Committee. The tone of his testimony was quite different from the strong language he had used on April 2 in response to Saddam Hussein's threats. "This administration," he said, "continues to oppose the imposition of sanctions, which would penalize American exporters and worsen our balance-of-payments deficit. Furthermore, I fail to see how sanctions could increase the possibility of our exercising a moderating influence on the actions of Iraq."

These words, from the man with responsibility for the Middle East, reflected the official stance of the State Department: for the moment there was no question of taking any firmer measures against Iraq. James Baker himself had come round to this position. While in Moscow the Secretary of State had met the Egyptian President, who was there on an official visit, and they had discussed Saddam Hussein's threats. Mubarak had advised Baker to adopt a low profile in the matter. That, according to him, was the best way to defuse the Iraqi leader's provocative tactics.

At the beginning of May two warning signals reached Washington—signals that no one in the administration was prepared to take seriously. The first was a surprising message to the White House from the CIA, stating that information in the Agency's possession pointed to "the possibility of an Iraqi attack on Kuwait." The White House had, in fact, been alerted to the possibility of an attack—but on Israel. The information was greeted with deep skepticism, and the official line remained unchanged.

Soon afterward a delegation of Israeli military and political experts arrived in Washington. Their analysis was a somber one: according to them, the moderate, reformist nature of the Iraqi regime was a smokescreen. Since February, they added, Saddam Hussein had consistently hardened his position: he had demanded the withdrawal of all American ships from the Gulf; he had urged the Arabs once again to use oil as a political weapon; and he had not only threatened to attack Israel, America's main ally in the region, but spoken of the possible use of chemical weapons. Finally, the constant massive buildup of his military machine was a further sign of his aggressive instincts.

The Israeli delegation obviously had some of the information that was passed on to the U.S. Ambassador to Israel, William A. Brown, at an Easter lunch in Jerusalem on April 15. Among those present at the lunch were the leader of the Labor Party, Shimon Peres, and General Ehud Barak, then deputy chief of the Israeli military forces. They were discussing Saddam Hussein's threat to launch chemical warfare attacks on Israel if Israel attacked Iraq when General Barak intervened: "Saddam Hussein's trying to fool the world. His plan isn't to attack Israel. You should look south from Iraq. That's where he is really looking." The general was referring to Kuwait and the United Arab Emirates.

The Israelis could not persuade anybody to share their anxieties. Some of those to whom they spoke attributed the tone of Iraqi statements to fear of a new Israeli raid on the chemical weapons factories, others to Saddam Hussein's wish to assert himself as the leader of the Arab world.

A strange blindness prevailed. The Iraqi President was seen as a man with a limited outlook on the world. He spoke no language other than Arabic and had paid only a single visit to the West: in 1975 he had gone to France to negotiate the purchase of a nuclear plant with the then Prime Minister, Jacques Chirac. He knew nothing of the United States and had once, in conversation with a Western visitor, expressed himself somewhat surprised to learn that the slightest criticism of the American President was not subject to laws as strict as those in Iraq, where such an "offense" was punishable by death.

Nobody in Washington seemed to understand that it was this very narrowness of vision that made Saddam Hussein dangerous. He behaved toward the rest of the world just as he acted in Iraq, ignoring the rules and restrictions governing international relations.

For many years he had had a remarkable observer working for him, his ambassador in Washington, Nizar Hamdoun, a respected diplomat who maintained regular contact with many high-ranking American officials. A month after the beginning of the crisis the *Wall Street Journal* even called him "the best foreign ambassador ever posted to the United States." Hamdoun had been recalled to Baghdad in 1987 to become deputy Foreign Minister, and his successor lacked both his contacts and his verve. One thing must have been obvious to Saddam Hussein from the exchanges of views he had had with officials such as Robert Dole, as well as from the contradictory positions adopted by Washington: the American leadership was irresolute and inclined more toward compromise than confrontation. This was to have serious consequences.

On May 21 an event occurred that helped to raise the tension by several notches. A young Israeli soldier killed seven unarmed Palestinians, and although the act was immediately condemned by the government in Jerusalem, unrest grew in the Occupied Territories. The Intifada, which had been marking time for months, now resumed, more violent than ever. This tragedy could not have come at a worse time. It happened exactly a week before the summit meeting of the Arab League that was due to be held in Baghdad in order to denounce the massive influx of Soviet Jews into Israel. Immediately after the slaughter Washington vetoed a PLO proposal at the United Nations to send international observers to the Occupied Territories. It was a stand that exacerbated still further the anti-American feelings that were being expressed virulently throughout the Arab world. There were bloody demonstrations in Jordan.

At a reception in the luxuriant gardens of his palace on May 24 King Hussein struck his guests as being deeply worried, though he circulated among the groups of guests, briefly joining in conversations, with a friendly word for everyone. He was elegantly and enthusiastically maintaining the fiction that his own power could render him immune to the upheavals around him. But nobody was fooled by his efforts, and as the evening progressed he revealed the extent to which he felt involved: "At the next summit in Baghdad I intend to demand financial aid not only for Jordan but also for the PLO." Saddam Hussein had earlier told him: "Leave it to me—I'll force them to pay."

The twenty-one Arab monarchs and heads of state who met in Baghdad on the morning of April 28 knew nothing of the drama that was unfolding. They had gathered to condemn the influx of Soviet Jews and to support Saddam Hussein's threats to destroy half of Israel. The true hero of the summit was the man who was playing the host. Not since Gamal Abdel Nasser had an Arab leader shown himself so capable of striking fear into the Jewish state.

The gathering, however, took a disconcerting turn when, to everyone's surprise, at the close of the opening session Saddam Hussein suggested holding a private meeting. King Fahd of Saudi Arabia tried to oppose the idea but, finding himself overruled by a large majority, was forced to concur. Saddam demanded that only heads of state be present. None of their colleagues was admitted. As Saddam said, "They don't need to hear the things we have to say."

He spoke in a very measured way, using the finest expressions of the Arabic language to make his point. Although the summit's topic was Soviet Jewish emigration to Israel, this was clearly not his theme at this private meeting. His target was the Gulf states. "They are extracting too much petrol and helping to keep prices at too low a level. Every time the price of a barrel drops by one dollar, Iraq loses $1 billion a year. You're virtually waging an economic war against my country."

The audience was stunned. Sheikh Zayed, President of the Federation of United Arab Emirates, was the first to speak for the defense. A tall man, draped in a white *abaya* with gold threads, he was a mediocre orator. Saddam Hussein replied: "I thank those Arab Emirates that have had a positive attitude toward us, but I also warn you that the shipments of arms and military equipment dispatched from Dubai to Iran during the war are things I haven't forgotten, and one day the reckoning will come."

Mubarak was leaning slightly forward, staring at the table and seething with inner rage. Gaddafi seemed amused as he let his eyes wander around the assembly. King Fahd of Saudi Arabia, who had developed friendly relations with Saddam Hussein, listened with real concern. He understood immediately that events in the region were becoming dangerous.

Saddam Hussein's speech, which was completely impromptu, was an unsettling mixture of aggressive demands, specific accusations and Arab stories used to point a moral. He spoke grandiloquently, increasingly punctuating his words with gestures. "Brothers, let me tell you an old legend that perhaps some of you know. One day disaster struck a little village, and all the villagers were asked to contribute something toward repairing the damage. In the village there lived a very poor man who had no possessions, and the other inhabitants decided not to ask him for anything. But the poor man approached them and said that he would feel ashamed not to contribute. He gave the other villagers the only thing he possessed, a copper pot. Well, at this summit that poor man is Iraq, but we shan't fail in our duty. We shall give $50 million to Jordan and $25 million to the PLO. That should help to exert moral pressure on those who might be tempted not to contribute. You all know the sacrifices we have accepted over the years while others fail to respect their agreements."

Here he looked directly at Jaber Al Sabah, the Emir of Kuwait, who was sitting a few yards away. The two men had long felt a deep antipathy toward each other.

"The quotas allocated by OPEC stipulated that Kuwait should not exceed a daily production of 1.5 million barrels; in actual fact, it has constantly extracted 2.1 million barrels a day. We are the ones to suffer. We Iraqis want to return to the economic situation that obtained in 1980, before the war against Iran. For the moment we urgently need $10 billion, as well as the cancellation of the $30 billion worth of debts to Kuwait, the Arab Emirates, and Saudi Arabia that we incurred during the war. Indeed, brother Arabs, it has to be clearly understood that we are today living through another conflict."

His tone had now become violent. "War doesn't mean just tanks, artillery or ships. It can take subtler and more insidious forms, such as the overproduction of oil, economic damage, and pressures to enslave a nation."

These last words were uttered amid an icy silence, which was broken by King Hussein, who said, "Nothing must be done to harm the economy of Iraq."

Now it was the turn of those who had been accused, notably the King of Saudi Arabia and, above all, the Emir of Kuwait. Both spoke in vague, general terms. They gave no words of encouragement and no promises of aid. What struck those present more than anything else was the strangely calm, almost indifferent, manner of Emir Jaber. In his attitude and that of his delegation, whom he quickly rejoined, there was something close to contempt for the Iraqi position and the demands that were being made.

OPEC's oil production had increased three times since the end of the Iran–Iraq War, each time at the insistence of the Kuwaitis who, in reply to the envoys sent by Baghdad, had never denied their involvement. The Kuwaitis liked their country to be known as "the Switzerland of the Middle East." They tended to forget that the Iraqis had a less impressive description for it: "A state made out of an oil well." They had also forgotten the attempted invasion launched by Saddam Hussein in 1973, when Iraqi troops had overrun the whole of the north of Kuwait before being briskly forced to retreat under pressure from the Arab world.

The Iraqi leaders implemented their policies with constant reference to five thousand years of glorious and romanticized history. They lived with dreams of a vanished empire whose power and prestige they hoped to restore. The Kuwaitis, on the other hand, were shrewd businessmen, living in the present, thinking only of their massive investments around the world. They believed that the Iraqi threats would go so far and no farther, for one obvious reason: never in the recent history of the Arab nation had one country invaded another. The Kuwaiti attitude could have been summed up perfectly by a proverb that has the ring of a death sentence: "A world without memory is destined to become a world without a future."

There was much discussion in the rooms and corridors of the

palace after Saddam Hussein's speech. One thing was clear to everybody, heads of state, ministers, and diplomatic advisers alike: the Iraqi regime and its leaders were going through a very difficult period. But only a few bold spirits went so far as to predict that the one solution open to Saddam Hussein was to seize Kuwait.

4

A Wolf and the Sheep

The first few weeks after May 30, 1990, were strangely calm, as if all the emotion and maneuvering had run out of steam.

In the middle of June an important European figure visiting Washington had occasion to talk to several people about the Iraqi question. "At that time," he was later to say, "nobody considered Iraq a threat. They saw it essentially as a major market for American products and as one of the few countries that still preferred American technology to that of its Japanese rival."

At the end of June Iraq's deputy Prime Minister, Saddoum Hammadi, embarked on a tour of the Gulf states. A refined, elegant man of sixty and a deeply devout Shi'ite, he was an economist who had received his education at the American University in Beirut and his Ph.D. from the University of Wisconsin. His journey took place a month before an important meeting of OPEC, and its purpose was to ask the Gulf leaders to accept lower quotas for oil production and to keep to them so that prices could return to their previous high level. On June 25 he arrived in Riyadh, where he urged King Fahd to support the Iraqi stand. Saudi Arabia was the one country in a position to promote the implementation of such a strategy.

In 1930 Ibn Seoud, the founder of Saudi Arabia, had confessed that he was "so poor that he did not even have a stone to lay his head on." Two years later the sole resource of the kingdom he had created by uniting the Bedouin tribes around him was the entrance fee paid by pilgrims to Mecca, and some years the receipts were so low that the country was on the verge of bankruptcy. In desperation Ibn Seoud appealed to the big oil companies, which were mostly British, to exploit his petroleum. "For a million dollars," he told a British businessman, "I'll give them all the concessions they want." Although the sum was absurdly low, nobody was interested in the proposal. There was so much oil available, especially that extracted by the Iraq Petroleum Company, that the major companies were agreed on one thing: in order to avoid yet more overproduction, Saudi oil was never to emerge from deep beneath the desert. The Arabian peninsula held no political or commercial appeal.

Within fifty years history had executed a complete turn about. Saudi Arabia had established itself as a petroleum giant with huge resources, able to produce 8 million to 10 million barrels a day. No important decision concerning petroleum policy could be made without the Saudis. But the present monarch, King Fahd, was hardly the man to make rapid or radical decisions. The kingdom was full of men of independent means whose wealth (more than $150 billion) had been acquired too quickly and easily and was reflected in cautious and sometimes irresolute regional policies.

Like most of the royal family, King Fahd regarded the Kuwaitis as arrogant and all too ready to proclaim themselves more adaptable and more modern than their Saudi neighbors. Where the Saudis—who, since the creation of their country, had considered it one vast mosque—turned their eyes toward Mecca, the Kuwaitis kept theirs on the West. Fahd was not unhappy to detect signs of anxiety in Kuwait City, but he also knew that Saddam Hussein's threats could eventually topple all the petroleum monarchies in the region.

He gave the Iraqi envoy, Saddoum Hammadi, a lengthy audience in his palace and listened carefully to his demands. A huge man with a round face, a little beard, and tired eyes (like most members of the Wahhabite dynasty since Ibn Seoud, he suffers from a hereditary eye disorder), he smiled affably at his guest and agreed that it might be a good idea to call a special meeting of OPEC to establish firm discipline among the oil-producing countries. But, he added immediately, in the same calm and amiable tone, there was no need to act hastily. The matter could be discussed by the oil ministers who were due to meet the following month in Geneva. For the moment, it was best to leave things as they were.

The King was a man slow in word and deed, for whom time seemed infinitely extensible. But time was precisely what the Iraqis lacked. For them, Fahd's response was hard to accept.

Saddoum Hammadi reminded both the king and Sheikh Zayed of Saddam Hussein's demand for a contribution of $10 billion. The replies he received were evasive. When he stopped in Kuwait, he made the same demand to Emir Jaber, who replied, "But that's absurd! We don't have such a large amount available."

During these discussions, Hammadi held two typewritten sheets of paper, stapled together, that detailed Kuwait's financial assets around the world. Its total investments exceeded $100 billion. In response to Hammadi's assessments of his country's wealth, the Emir proposed paying the sum of $500 million, spread over three years, as an act of charity to Iraq. "Let's agree about our borders," he went on. "Let's ratify those, and then we can talk about other things."

No sooner had Hammadi returned to Baghdad than he learned

of the Kuwaiti Petroleum Minister's announcement that his country was to maintain her surplus production until October. This decision, coupled with the Saudi rejection of a special meeting of OPEC, convinced Saddam Hussein that there was, as he told one of his colleagues, "an attempt to bring Iraq to her knees."

On July 16, Iraq's Foreign Minister, Tariq Aziz, arrived in Tunis to attend a meeting of the Arab League. A stout man of sixty, with severe glasses and a thick salt-and-pepper moustache, he was one of the few Christians to occupy a high position in Iraq's ruling apparatus. (His real first name was Johanna.) Amiable in manner, he could convey total intransigence with subtlety and courtesy. Virtually Saddam Hussein's traveling salesman on the international scene, he had represented Iraq in all its most delicate negotiations, whether discussing with the countries of Europe the recycling of its debts or pressing for further access to credit for purchasing arms. Zealously, skillfully, and sometimes sternly, he gave voice to Saddam Hussein's thoughts and wishes.

The meeting had been called to rally the support of the Arab nations for the PLO. Yasser Arafat, who had moved his organization towards a more moderate position, accepting the independence of Israel and starting a dialogue with the United States, was finding himself isolated again. On June 20 the United States had broken off its diplomatic conversations with the PLO in retaliation for a failed terrorist attack on an Israeli beach by Abul Abbas on May 30, 1990. Abbas was the man who had already demonstrated his terrorist abilities by masterminding the hijacking of the Italian ship *Achille Lauro* in 1985. Although a terrorist, Abul Abbas was still a member of the PLO's Fatah Council. The U.S. had insisted that Arafat fire him from the post and disown the failed attack. But Arafat had not done so.

Many Arab countries had not come to the Arab League summit in Tunis on that day, which angered Arafat. But the fact that Tariq Aziz was present was not surprising. His boss, Saddam

Hussein, had played an important role in convincing Arafat to adopt a new, moderate, position and to start talks with the U.S. Speaking to those present, Arafat attacked some of the nations that had not shown up, particularly Saudi Arabia and Egypt. He closed the speech saying, "This is a big problem, but many Arab countries don't care. What are they doing? Are they trying to sort out the price of potatoes?" Arafat walked out of the room, and the meeting ended.

Tariq Aziz walked over to the Secretary-General of the Arab League and told him: "I've brought an important memorandum that has to be distributed to all the members of the Arab League. We must have a meeting tomorrow morning." Klibi agreed. Walking out, Tariq Aziz had a conversation with his Jordanian counterpart, Marwan Al Qasim. He told him about the memo and added: "We are convinced that certain states are engaged in a genuine conspiracy against us. Let me tell you that our country won't be brought to its knees, that our women won't be forced into prostitution, and that our children won't be deprived of their food."

Al Qasim was shocked. He told Tariq Aziz: "You're in the process of walking into a trap. You have to be careful."

Tariq Aziz didn't reply and walked out.

The next morning, July 17, Aziz showed up at Chadli Klibi's office with the Iraqi ambassador to Tunisia. He handed the memorandum over to Klibi. Klibi, a Tunisian diplomat with the appearance of a shy intellectual, was a level-headed man. The memorandum shocked him. It was in effect a declaration of war by Iraq against Kuwait. The grievances aired no longer concentrated only on the overproduction of petroleum. Iraq accused Kuwait of installing military posts on its territory and stealing more than $2.4 billion worth of oil extracted from the Rumailah field, which Iraq claimed as its own. Kuwait and the United Arab

Emirates were also named as part of a "Zionist and Imperialist plot against the Arab nation."

Klibi decided to try to hold off distributing the memorandum. He told Aziz he wanted twenty-four hours of consultation with Kuwait and Saudi Arabia before the memo was distributed to other Arab nations. He also said he wanted to talk immediately to Saddam Hussein. Aziz interrupted him. "You can't talk to Saddam Hussein. He is in the process of delivering a very important speech." Later in the day Klibi would learn that the speech included some of the threats that were in the memorandum. Aziz was not in a mood to negotiate with Klibi. He was obviously there under firm orders from his President. The meeting was over.

When Aziz left, Klibi immediately sent a copy of the memorandum to the Kuwaiti embassy in Tunis. The Ambassador called back an hour later and asked Klibi if he was going to distribute the memo. The head of the Arab League said he had no choice. He told the Ambassador to notify the Kuwaiti Foreign Minister, Sheikh Sabah Al Ahmad, and said he wanted to talk to him, the Emir of Kuwait, and the Crown Prince.

When Sheikh Sabah received the memorandum he seemed "punch-drunk," according to an eyewitness. The Iraqis were accusing him of being an agent in the pay of the Americans. He decided to cancel all his engagements.

Since the end of May the Hong Kong and Singapore money markets had been aware of some unusual movements. The Kuwait Investment Office (KIO), the London-based body that managed Kuwait's huge worldwide investments, for no apparent reason, had sold off a number of major assets. A few days after the Tunis meeting, which began on July 19, the KIO began a process of complete withdrawal from the Asian markets in order to invest instead in liquid assets. The Kuwaiti dealers had acted quickly, but also with remarkable discretion, to prevent the news from getting out and provoking a mini-crash on the markets where the KIO was a significant presence.

While Tariq Aziz was meeting with Chadll Klibi on July 17, it was the anniversary of the Iraqi Revolution. Saddam Hussein mounted the rostrum surrounded by the members of the Revolution Command Council, all of them in uniform. Every time the President appeared in public, Baghdad was almost in a state of siege, but that day security was even tighter than usual.

"Thanks to our new weapons," Saddam announced in a speech that was later broadcast on radio, "the imperialists can no longer launch a military attack against us, so they have chosen to wage an economic guerrilla war with the help of those agents of imperialism, the leaders of the Gulf states. Their policy of keeping oil prices at a low level is a poisoned dagger planted in Iraq's back." For the first time he mentioned the threat of military intervention: "If words fail to protect us, we will have no choice other than to go into action to reestablish the correct state of affairs and restore our rights."

That same day the first Iraqi troops began to move toward the Kuwaiti border.

Late in the afternoon of July 18, the Kuwaiti cabinet met. Getting out of their luxury American limousines as the sun began to sink into the sea, all the ministers looked tense. The threat was there, not many miles away, in the tangible form of Iraqi T62 tanks moving toward their country. Although they were aware of the danger, most of them preferred to believe that the situation was still salvageable.

Emir Jaber was the last to arrive, accompanied by Crown Prince Sheikh Saad Al-Abdullah Al Sabah, who was also the Prime Minister. The Prince had just returned from Saudi Arabia, where King Fahd had offered to act as mediator. The Emir and his Prime Minister had exchanged views before the meeting. Both considered it possible that Iraq would attack their country, but they believed that the operation would be limited to the disputed border areas. Nobody was prepared to admit that Kuwait was a peaceful parenthesis about to be closed.

The purpose of the cabinet meeting was to agree on a response to the memorandum delivered by Tariq Aziz in which Kuwait was accused of stealing $2.4 billion worth of oil from Iraq. But the many speeches revealed nothing so much as the anxiety and confusion that everyone was feeling.

The first to speak was Ali Khalifa Al Sabah, formerly Petroleum Minister, now an enterprising Finance Minister, a man with the manners of a Western banker and a respected figure within the international financial community. "I think," he said, "that Iraq is trying to save its economy and is blaming the Gulf states for its own failures. But we mustn't delude ourselves. Iraq isn't going to change, even after the OPEC meeting in Geneva. Things will continue to escalate."

Khalifa Al Sabah's statement met with approving nods from several of his colleagues. The proposal he then made was somewhat less realistic. He suggested that a solution should be sought through the Gulf Cooperation Council, a defense body whose members were Kuwait, the United Arab Emirates, Oman, Qatar, Bahrain, and Saudi Arabia—in other words, all the region's reigning monarchies that Iraq had named as its enemies.

Some of those who spoke, such as the minister in charge of Parliament and the minister responsible for cabinet affairs, clung to the idea that the Iraqi threats had only one purpose— "to extort money, lots of money, from Kuwait." One of them even added, "We must keep calm." Salman Al Mutawa, the minister in charge of planning, went so far as to consider the memorandum "a sign of weakness that could easily be answered."

But these opinions did not represent the majority view. It was not enough for Defense Minister Sheikh Naiwal Al Sabah to reject Iraq's accusations by maintaining that it was the Iraqis who had installed military equipment across the border. What the Emir really wanted to know was how serious the Iraqi threat was. Sheikh Al Ahmad Al Sabah, head of the diplomatic service, and the man who had been stunned by the memorandum and by Tariq Aziz's accusations, replied: "There is a possibility the Iraqis will attack. The situation on the border is explosive. We are engaged in intense diplomatic discussions with our brothers in the Gulf Cooperation Council."

Negotiation: that was the word on everyone's lips. It was the last hope of averting disaster. They had forgotten the many meetings between envoys of Iraq and Kuwait, at which the latter had casually but firmly rejected the demands of their opposite numbers.

"I think," said the Crown Prince, "that the Iraqis may take military action but that the operation will be limited to the borders, in the area of Ritqa and Quasar."

As the meeting wore on, those present began to feel almost reassured, and they paid little attention to what was the most noteworthy speech of all, that of Justice Minister Dhari-Othman: "The Iraqi memorandum is just the beginning. God only knows how far they will go. The question of oil prices is only a pretext. In reality, Iraq is a wolf and we are the sheep."

The meeting went on to discuss the economic question. Here things become less clear-cut. Should those present accede to Iraq's request for $10 billion and the cancellation of all existing debts?

No decision was taken, though time was pressing. Sheikh Al

Ahmad Al Sabah was given the task of organizing in Kuwait City an emergency meeting of the Gulf Cooperation Council with the purpose of calling for the intervention of the Arab League. No military measures were adopted.

While this meeting was going on, Chadli Klibi got a message in Tunis telling him that the Kuwaiti government was sending him a Swiss charter plane to fly him to Kuwait to see their leaders. On arriving in Kuwait City, he was immediately taken to the Palace to see the Emir. The Emir expressed complete surprise at the memorandum Tariq Aziz had handed over to Klibi several days earlier. "What is the problem? This memorandum is tough. It is not true. We gave Saddam Hussein a lot of money and oil during the war with Iran." Klibi would later be told by an assistant of the Emir that the Kuwaitis had given the Iraqis 300,000 barrels of oil a day and $17 billion during the war. He was also told that this information had never been released publicly because the Kuwaitis were afraid that it would anger Iran and cause problems. As the meeting closed, the Emir told Klibi: "Try to solve the problem. We're ready for dialogue to solve the problem."

Klibi decided that his next step would be to fly to Baghdad. But, just as he was leaving the hotel, he learned that the Saudi Foreign Minister, Prince Faisal, was on his way to the Iraqi capital. He decided to stay in Kuwait, confident that Prince Faisal would stop there and brief him on his meetings with Saddam Hussein.

What the Kuwaitis had not told Klibi was another factor in their mentality. It is entirely possible that Kuwaiti leaders thought they had a last card up their sleeves: the support of the United States. First, they had not forgotten that during the Iraq–Iran war the Americans had allowed the Kuwaiti government to put American flags on its oil tankers—a clear sign that they were standing by Kuwait. There is also a strange document dated November 22, 1989, that the Iraqis claim they discovered in the Kuwaiti Foreign Ministry after they took over Kuwait. The CIA spokesman, Peter Earnest, released an official statement on October 30, 1990, saying the document was a forgery. But the statement conceded that Sheikh Al Sabah, the deputy director of Kuwaiti State Security, did pay a visit to the CIA director, Judge William Webster, in November of 1989, as the document had indicated. The Iraqi government continued to maintain that the document was accurate. Anyway, it was interesting to read. The document is a memorandum alleged to have been drawn up by Fahd Hakmad Al Fahd, Kuwait's director of State Security, addressed to the Interior Minister. The fifth paragraph of the document states:

We agreed with the American side that it was important to take advantage of the deteriorating economic situation in Iraq in order to put pressure on that country's government to delineate our common border. The Central Intelligence Agency gave us its view of appropriate means of pressure, saying that broad co-operation should be initiated between us on the condition that such activities are co-ordinated at a high level.

The director of State Security also mentions a six-day trip to Washington, November 12–18, in the course of which he held several top-secret meetings with the higher echelons of the CIA. The agency expressed dissatisfaction with the performance of the Kuwaiti Royal Guard, whose job it was to protect the Emir. The latter had been the target of several assassination attempts, and, according to the memorandum, the CIA was prepared to train and maintain 123 people, selected by the Kuwaiti authorities, who would in the future be entrusted with the task of ensuring the safety of the Emir and the Crown Prince.

Had the Kuwaitis, convinced that Washington would support them all the way, gone too far? The leaders of the Emirate had long been certain of U.S. support, especially since 1987, when (as previously mentioned) Kuwaiti tankers had been placed under the American flag.

That day the Iraqi Parliament announced the decision—obviously a unanimous one—to name Saddam Hussein President for life.

On July 24 information reached CIA headquarters that two Iraqi divisions had left their bases to take up position on the Kuwaiti border.

That morning Hosni Mubarak arrived in Baghdad on a mission of mediation. He had been chosen for this task by the Arab League—not a particularly auspicious choice, given the mutual suspicion that existed between Saddam Hussein and the Egyptian President.

"As long as discussions last between Iraq and Kuwait," Saddam told his opposite number, "I won't use force. I won't intervene with force before I have exhausted all the possibilities for negotiation. But don't tell that to the Kuwaitis, Brother Mubarak. It'll only make them conceited."

Immediately after this meeting Mubarak flew to Kuwait, where he reported to the Emir what the Iraqi President had said—but only in part. "Don't worry, Excellency. I've had it from the mouth of Saddam Hussein himself that he won't send troops and that he has no intention of attacking Kuwait."

He declined to add "as long as negotiations last." He passed on the same truncated message to Washington.

On July 25, Saddam summoned the American Ambassador, April Glaspie. Informed only an hour in advance, she had no time to ask the State Department for instructions. She was tense by 1 P.M., when she entered the Iraqi leader's office for her first private meeting with him. The conversation that followed was surprising, even disconcerting. A transcript of it was obtained by the ABC television network and is a document of major importance, containing many clues, some of them involuntary, that are worth decoding.*

Saddam Hussein had Tariq Aziz with him. He greeted the Ambassador in a friendly manner, motioned her to sit down, and at once began: "I have summoned you today to hold comprehensive political discussions with you. This is a message to President Bush." The president continued:

You know that we did not have relations with the U.S. until 1984, and you know the circumstances and reasons that caused them to be severed. The decision to establish relations with the U.S. were taken in 1980, during the two months prior to the war between us and Iran.

When the war started, and to avoid misinterpretation, we postponed the establishment of relations, hoping that the war would end soon.

But because the war lasted for a long time, and to emphasize the fact that we are a non-aligned country, it was important to reestablish relations with the U.S. And we chose to do this in 1984.

It is natural to say that the U.S. is not like Britain, for example, with the latter's historic relations with Middle Eastern countries, including Iraq. In addition, there were no relations between Iraq and the U.S. between 1967 and 1984. One can conclude that it would be difficult for the U.S. to have a full understanding of many matters in Iraq.

*The transcript of this meeting has been translated from the Arabic by Adel Darwish.

46

When relations were reestablished we hoped for a better understanding and for better cooperation because we too do not understand the background of many American decisions.

We dealt with each other during the war and we had dealings on various levels. The most important of those levels was that of the foreign ministers.

We had hoped for a better common understanding and a better chance of cooperation to benefit both our peoples and the rest of the Arab nations.

But these better relations have suffered from various rifts. The worst of these was in 1986, only two years after establishing relations, with what was known as "Irangate," which happened during the year that Iran occupied the Fao peninsula.

It was natural then to say that old relations and the complexity of mutual interests could absorb many mistakes. But when interests are limited and relations are not that old, then there isn't a deep understanding and mistakes may have a negative effect. Sometimes the effect of an error can be more serious than the error itself.

Despite that, we accepted the apology, via his envoy, of the American President regarding "Irangate," and we wiped the slate clean. And we shouldn't unearth the past except when new events remind us that old mistakes were not just a matter of coincidence.

Our suspicions increased after we liberated the Fao peninsula. The media began to involve themselves in our politics. And our suspicions began to surface anew because we began to question whether the U.S. felt uneasy with the outcome of the war when we liberated our land.

It was clear to us that certain parties in the United States—and I don't say the President himself but certain parties who had links with the intelligence community and with the State Department, and I don't say the Secretary of State himself—did not like the fact that we had liberated our land. Some parties began to prepare studies entitled "Who will succeed Saddam Hussein?" They began to contact Gulf states to make them fear Iraq, to persuade them not to give Iraq economic aid. And we have evidence of these activities.

Iraq came out of the war burdened with $40 million in debt, excluding the aid given by Arab states, some of whom consider that too to be a debt, although they knew—and you knew too—that without Iraq they would not have had these sums and the future of the region would have been entirely different.

We began to face the policy of the drop in the price of oil. Then we saw that the United States talks constantly of democracy but has no time for the other point of view. Then the campaign against Saddam Hussein was started by the official American media. The United States thought that the situation in Iraq was like that in Poland, Romania or Czechoslovakia. We were disturbed by this campaign, but we were not too anxious because we had hoped that, in a few months, those who are decision-makers in America would have a chance to find out the facts and judge whether this media campaign had had any affect on the lives of Iraqis. We hoped that soon the American authorities would make the correct decision regarding their relations with Iraq. Those with good relations can sometimes afford to disagree.

But when planned and deliberate policy forces the price of oil down without good commercial reasons, that means another war against Iraq because military war kills people by spilling their blood, and economic war destroys their humanity by depriving them of a chance to enjoy a good standard of living. As you know, we spilled rivers of blood in a war that lasted eight years, but we did not lose our humanity. Iraqis have a right to live proudly; we do not accept that anyone may injure Iraqi pride or the Iraqi right to enjoy high standards of living.

For Saddam Hussein the actions of the Gulf states regarding the price of oil amounted to a genuine declaration of war.

Kuwait and the UAE (United Arab Emirates) were at the forefront of this policy aimed at lowering Iraq's position and depriving its people of higher economic standards. And you know that our relations with the Emirates and Kuwait had been good. On top of all that, while we were busy waging war the state of Kuwait began to expand at the expense of our territory.

He was now clearly indicating Kuwait as his main target.

You may say that this is propaganda, but I would direct your attention to a document that defines the Military Patrol Line, which is the border line endorsed by the Arab States League in 1961 that military patrols may not cross [the Iraq–Kuwait border].

But go and look for yourselves. You will see the Kuwaiti border patrols, the Kuwaiti farms, the Kuwaiti oil installations—all built as close to this line as possible to establish that land as Kuwaiti territory.

Since then [1961], the Kuwaiti government has been stable, while the Iraqi government has undergone many changes. Even after 1968 [when the Ba'ath party came to power], and for ten years afterwards, we were too busy with our own problems, first in the north [the war against the Kurds, then the 1973 war [Yom Kippur], and other problems. Then came the war with Iran, which started ten years ago.

We believe that the United States must understand that people who live in luxury and economic security can reach an understanding with the United States about what are legitimate joint interests, but the starved and the economically deprived cannot reach the same understanding.

We do not accept threats from anyone because we do not threaten anyone. But we say clearly that we hope that the U.S. will not entertain too many illusions and will seek new friends rather than increase the number of its enemies.

I have read American statements speaking of friends in the area. Of course, it is the right of everyone to choose their friends. We can have no objections. But, you know, you are not the ones who protected your friends during the war with Iran. I assure you, had the Iranians overrun the region. American troops would not have stopped them except by the use of nuclear weapons.

I do not belittle you, but I hold this view because I have taken the geography and nature of American society into account. Yours is a society that cannot accept 10,000 dead in one battle.

You know that Iran agreed to the ceasefire, but that was not because the United States had bombed one of its oil platforms after the liberation of the Fao. Is this Iraq's reward for its role in securing the stability of the region and for protecting it from an unprecedented flood?

So what can America mean when it says it will now protect its friends? It can mean only prejudice against Iraq.

This stance, plus certain maneuvres and statements that have been made, has encouraged the UAE and Kuwait to disregard Iraqi rights.

I say to you clearly that Iraq's rights, which are mentioned in the memorandum, we will assert one by one. This may not happen now, or in a month's time, or at the end of a year, but we will assert all our rights. We are not the kind of people who will relinquish their rights. There is no historic authority or legitimacy, or need, for the UAE and Kuwait to deprive us of our rights. If they are needy, we too are needy.

The United States must have a better understanding of the situation and declare with whom it wants to have relations and who its enemies are. But it should not make enemies simply because others have different points of view regarding the Arab–Israeli conflict.

We understand clearly America's statement that it wants an easy flow of oil. We understand America when it says that it seeks friendship with the states in the region and wishes to promote their joint interests. But we cannot understand the attempt to encourage some parties to harm Iraq's interests.

The United States wants to secure the flow of oil. This is understandable and understood. But it must not deploy methods of which the United States says it disapproves— that is, the flexing of muscles and pressure. If you use pressure, we will deploy both pressure and force.

We know that you can harm us, although we do not threaten you. But we too could harm you. Everyone can cause damage according to his ability and size. We cannot come all the way to you in the United States, but individual Arabs may reach you.

Untroubled by diplomatic niceties, Saddam Hussein was threatening the United States with a wave of terrorist attacks. To make matters even clearer, he added:

> You can come to Iraq with aircraft and missiles, but do not push us to the point at which we cease to care. When we feel that you want to injure our pride and destroy the Iraqis' chance of a high standard of living, we will cease to care, and death will be our choice. Then we would not care if you fired a hundred missiles for each missile we fired because, without pride, life would have no value.

This was a warning to President Bush that Saddam was ready for a war against America, even though he knew that he would probably lose.

> It is not reasonable to ask our people to bleed rivers of blood for eight years, then to tell them, "Now you have to accept aggression from Kuwait, the UAE, the U.S. or Israel."
>
> We do not put all these countries in the same boat. We are hurt and upset that such disagreement is taking place between us and Kuwait and the UAE. The solution must be found within an Arab framework and through direct bilateral relations. We do not place America among our enemies; we place it where we want our friends to be, and we try to be friends. But repeated American statements last year made it apparent that America did not regard us as friends. Well, the Americans are free.
>
> When we seek friendship, we want pride, liberty and the right to choose.
>
> We want to deal according to our status as we deal with others according to their status.

We consider others' interests while we look after our own. And we expect others to consider our interests while they are protecting their own. What does it mean that the Zionist War Minister has been summoned to the United States now? What do they mean, these fiery statements coming out of Israel during the past few days and the talk of war being expected now more than at any other time?

No doubt still haunted by the traumatic bombing of the Osiraq nuclear plant, Saddam Hussein had no hesitation in revealing to the Ambassador his fear of an imminent Israeli attack, perhaps supported by the United States.

We don't want war because we know what war means. But do not push us to consider war as the only means by which we can live proudly and provide our people with a good living.

We know that the United States has nuclear weapons. But we are all determined either to live as proud men or to die. We do not believe that there is a single honest man on earth who would not understand what I mean.

We do not ask you to solve our problems. I have said that our Arab problems will be solved among ourselves. But do not encourage anyone to take action that is greater than his status warrants.

I do not believe that anyone would suffer as a result of making friends with Iraq. In my opinion, the American President has made no mistakes regarding the Arabs, although his decision to freeze the dialogue with the PLO was wrong. It appears, however, that this decision was made to appease the Zionist lobby or was a piece of strategy designed to cool Zionist anger before trying again. I hope that the latter conclusion is the correct one. But we will carry on saying that it was the wrong decision.

You are appeasing the usurper in so many ways: economically, politically, and militarily, as well as through the media. When will the time come when, for every three conciliatory statements you make to the usurper, you praise the Arabs just once? When will humanity sieze its chance to seek a just American solution that would balance the human rights of 200 million human beings with the rights of three million Jews? We want friendship but we will chase no one for it. We reject armed hostility from any quarter. If we are faced with hostility we will resist. This is our right, whether the aggression comes from America, or the UAE, or Kuwait, or Israel. But I do not place all these states on the same level. Israel stole Arab land, supported by the U.S. The UAE and Kuwait do not support Israel. Anyway they are Arabs. But when they try to weaken Iraq, they are helping the enemy, and then Iraq has the right to defend itself.

At this stage of the interview, to add weight to his plea, Saddam Hussein recalled two precedents that should have given America pause for thought.

In 1974 I met with Idriss, the son of Mullah Mustafa Barzani [the late Kurdish leader]. He sat in the very seat in which you are sitting now. He came to ask me to postpone the implementation of autonomy in Iraqi Kurdistan, which was agreed on March 11, 1970. My reply was, "We are determined to fulfill our obligations. You also have to stick to your agreement." When I sensed that Barzani had evil intentions I said to him, "Give my regards to your father and tell him that Saddam Hussein says the following." I then explained the balance of power to him, with the aid of statistics, exactly as I explained it to the Iranians in my open letters to them during the war. I ended the conversation by summarizing the consequences in one sentence: "If we fight, we shall win." Do you know why? I explained all the reasons to him, including one political reason. They [the Kurds in 1974] depended on our disagreement with the Shah of Iran. [The Kurds were financed by Iran.] The source of the Iranian conflict was Iran's claim to half of the Shatt al-Arab waterway. If we could keep the whole of Iraq with Shatt al-Arab, we would make no concessions. But if forced to choose between half of Shatt al-Arab or the whole of Iraq, then we would give away the Shatt al-Arab to preserve the whole of Iraq just as we wish it to be.

We hope that you are not going to push events to the point at which we will be obliged to recall the choice that we were forced to make in our relations with Iran. After that [the meeting with Barzani's son] we gave away half of Shatt al-Arab [under the terms of the 1975 Algeria agreement]. And Barzani died and was buried outside Iraq, and he lost his war.

The Iraqi leader addressed the U.S. Ambassador directly:

We hope we are not being pushed into this. All that lies between relations with Iran is Shatt al-Arab. When we are faced with a choice between Iraq living proudly and Shatt al-Arab, we will negotiate using the wisdom we acquired in 1975. Just as Barzani lost his historic chance, others will lose their chance too.

Saddam Hussein concluded this historical account by stating bluntly:

> With regard to President Bush, I hope the President will read this himself and will not leave it in the hands of a gang in the State Department. I exclude the Secretary of State and Kelly because I know him and have exchanged views with him.

The American Ambassador was finally able to reply:

> I thank you, Mr. President, and it is a great pleasure for a diplomat to meet and talk directly with the President. I clearly understand your message. We studied history at school. They taught us to say, "Freedom or death."
>
> I think you know well that we as a people have our own experience of colonialists.
>
> Mr. President, you mentioned during this meeting many things that I cannot comment on on behalf of my government. But, with your permission, I will comment on two points. You spoke of friendship, and I believe it was clear from the letters sent by our President to you on the occasion of your National Day that he emphasizes—

Saddam Hussein interrupted: "He was kind, and his expressions met with our regard and respect."

The Ambassador continued. "As you know, he directed the United States administration to reject the suggestion of implementing trade sanctions."

Saddam Hussein said, smiling, "There is nothing left for us to buy from America except wheat. Every time we want to buy something, they say it is forbidden. I am afraid that one day you will say, 'You are going to make gunpowder out of wheat.' "

The Ambassador hastened to reassure him. "I have a direct instruction from the President to seek better relations with Iraq."

"But how?" asked Saddam Hussein. "We too have this desire, but matters are running contrary to this desire."

The Ambassador replied, "This is less likely to happen the more we talk. For example, you mentioned the issue of the article published by the American Information Agency, and that was sad, and a formal apology was offered."

In his most charming manner Saddam Hussein leaned toward her. "Your stance is generous. We are Arabs. It is enough for us that someone says, 'I am sorry. I have made a mistake.' Then we carry on. But the media campaign continued. And it is full of stories. If the stories were true, no one would get upset. But we understand from its continuation that there is determination [to harm relations]."

The Ambassador fully agreed with him:

I saw the Diane Sawyer program on ABC. And what happened in that program was cheap and unjust. And this is a real picture of what happens in the American media—even to American politicians themselves. These are the methods that the Western media employ. I am pleased that you add your voice to the diplomats who stand up to the media because your appearance in the media, even for five minutes, would help us to make the American people understand Iraq. This would increase mutual understanding. If the American President had control of the media, his job would be much easier.

Mr. President, I want to say that President Bush wants not only better and deeper relations with Iraq but also an

Iraqi contribution to peace and prosperity in the Middle East. President Bush is an intelligent man. He is not going to declare an economic war against Iraq.

You are right. It is true what you say that we do not want higher prices for oil. But I would ask you to examine the possibility of not charging too high a price for oil.

The President said in a conciliatory tone, "We do not want too high prices for oil. And may I remind you that in 1974 I gave Tariq Aziz the idea for an article he wrote that criticized the policy of keeping oil prices high. It was the first Arab article that expressed this view."

Tariq Aziz then spoke for the first time. "Our policy in OPEC opposes sudden jumps in oil prices."

The President said, "Twenty-five dollars a barrel is not a high price."

The Ambassador replied, "We have many Americans who would like to see the price go above $25 because they come from oil-producing states." This was another green light, giving Saddam Hussein to believe that the Ambassador, and through her the President, agreed with his demands for higher prices.

The President said: "The price at one stage had dropped to twelve dollars a barrel, and a reduction in the modest Iraqi budget of $6–7 billion is a disaster."

The American Ambassador responded:

I think I understand this. I have lived here for years. I admire your extraordinary efforts to rebuild your country. I know you need funds. We understand that, and our opinion is that you should have the opportunity to rebuild your country. But we have no opinion on Arab–Arab conflicts, like your border disagreement with Kuwait.

I was in the American Embassy in Kuwait during the late 1960s. The instruction we had during that period was that we should express no opinion on this issue and that the issue was not associated with America. James Baker has directed our official spokesman to emphasize this instruction. We hope you can solve this problem using any suitable methods via Kalibi [Secretary-General, Arab States League] or President Mubarak. All that we hope is that these issues will be solved quickly. With regard to all of this, can I ask you to understand how the issue appears to us? [Another green light: the Iraq–Kuwait border dispute is none of our business.]

My assessment after twenty-five years' service in this area is that your objective must have strong backing from your Arab brothers. I now speak of oil. But you, Mr. President, have fought a horrific and painful war. Frankly, we can see only that you have deployed massive troops in the south. Normally that would not be any of our business. But when this happens in the context of what you said on your National Day, when we read the details in the two letters of the Foreign Minister, when we see the Iraqi point of view that the measures taken by the UAE and Kuwait are, in the final analysis, tantamount to military aggression against Iraq, then it is reasonable for me to be concerned. And for this reason I have received an instruction to ask you, in the spirit of friendship, not in the spirit of confrontation, about your intentions.

I simply describe the concern of my government. I do not mean that the situation is a simple one, but our concern is simple.

The President said:

We do not ask people not to be concerned when peace is at issue. This is a noble human feeling, which we all feel. It is natural for you as a superpower to be concerned. But what we ask is that you do not express your concern in a way that could make an aggressor believe that he is getting support for his aggression.

We want to find a just solution that will give us our rights but not deprive others of theirs. But at the same time we want others to know that our patience is running out regarding their action, which is harming even the milk our children drink, and the pension of the widow who lost her husband during the war, and the pensions of the orphans who lost their parents.

As a country, we have the right to prosper. We have lost many opportunities as a consequence of the war, and others should value Iraq's role in their own protection. Even this Iraqi [the President pointed at the interpreter] feels bitter, as do all other Iraqis. We are not aggressors, and we do not tolerate aggression either. We sent them envoys and handwritten letters. We tried everything. We asked the Servant of the Two Shrines, King Fahd, to hold a four-member summit, but he suggested a meeting between the Oil Ministers. We agreed. And, as you know, the meeting took place in Jeddah. They reached an agreement that did not express what we wanted, but we concurred.

Only two days after the meeting, the Kuwaiti Oil Minister made a statement that contradicted the agreement. We also discussed the issue during the Baghdad summit. I told the Arab Kings and Presidents that certain brothers were fighting an economic war against us, that not all wars involve weapons, and that we regard this kind of war as a military action against us. Because if the capability of our army is reduced, then, if Iran renewed the war, it could achieve goals that it could not achieve before. And if we lowered our defenses, then this might encourage Israel to attack us. I said that before the Arab Kings and Presidents. Only I did not mention Kuwait and the UAE by name because they were my guests.

Before this I had sent them envoys reminding them that our war had included their defense. Therefore the aid they gave us should not be regarded as a debt. We did more than the United States would have done against someone who attacked its interests.

I talked about this matter with a number of other Arab states. I explained the situation to Brother King Fahd a few times, through envoys and on the telephone. I talked with Brother King Hussein and with Sheikh Zaid after the conclusion of the summit. I walked with the Sheikh to the plane when he was leaving Mosul. He told me, "Just wait until I get home." But after he had reached his destination the statements that came from there were very bad—not from him, but from his Minister of Oil.

Also, after the Jeddah agreement we received some intelligence that they were talking of sticking to the agreement for two months only. Then they would change their policy. Now tell us: if the American President found himself in this situation, what would he do? I said it was very difficult for me to talk about these issues in public. But we must tell the Iraqi people, who face economic difficulties, who was responsible for that.

In response to these harsh words, the Ambassador preferred to change the subject. "I spent four beautiful years in Egypt."

The President replied, "The Egyptian people are kind and good and ancient. The oil people are supposed to help the Egyptian people, but they are mean beyond belief. It is painful to admit it, but some of them are disliked by Arabs because of their greed."

"Mr. President, it would be helpful if you could give us an assessment of the effort made by your Arab brothers and whether they have achieved anything."

"On this subject, we agreed with President Mubarak that the Prime Minister of Kuwait would meet with the Deputy Chairman of the Revolution Command Council in Saudi Arabia because the Saudis initiated contact with us, aided by President Mubarak's efforts. He telephoned me a short while ago to say the Kuwaitis have agreed to that suggestion."

The Ambassador said, relieved, "Congratulations."

The President continued, "A protocol meeting will be held in Saudi Arabia. Then the meeting will be transferred to Baghdad for deeper discussion directly between Kuwait and Iraq. We hope that we will reach some conclusion. We hope that the long-term view and the real interests at stake will overcome Kuwaiti greed."

"May I ask you when you expect Sheikh Saad to come to Baghdad?"

The President replied, "I suppose it will be on Saturday, or Monday at the latest [July 28 or 30]. I told Brother Mubarak that the agreement should be in Baghdad on Saturday or Sunday. You know that Brother Mubarak's visit have always been a good omen."

"This is good news. Congratulations."

Saddam Hussein was no longer trying to play his cards close to his chest:

Brother President Mubarak told me they were scared. They said troops were only 20 kilometers [about 12 miles] north of the Arab League line [the Kuwaiti border]. I said to him that regardless of what is there, whether they are police, border guards, or army, and regardless of how many are there and what they are doing, assure the Kuwaitis and give them our word that we are not going to do anything until we meet with them. If, when we meet, we see that there is hope, nothing will happen. But if we are unable to find a solution, then it will be natural that Iraq will not accept death, even though wisdom is above everything else. There you have good news.

Tariq Aziz said, "This is a journalistic exclusive."

What April Glaspie was to retain from the whole interview was this optimistic conclusion, forgetting all the threats and warnings with which Saddam Hussein had peppered his statements. Taking her leave, the Ambassador assured her host one last time that his message would reach the man for whom it was intended: "I am planning to go to the United States next Monday [July 30]. I hope I will meet with President Bush in Washington next week. I thought to postpone my trip because of the difficulties we are facing. But now I will fly on Monday."

At the end of the meeting they exchanged greetings and good wishes.

Chadli Klibi, who had waited forty-eight hours in Kuwait for the Saudi Foreign Minister to brief him on his meetings in Baghdad, finally left Kuwait City, frustrated that the Saudi diplomat had never shown up. When the meeting between Saddam Hussein and April Glaspie ended, Tariq Aziz, who had participated in the meeting, drove over to the Al Rashid Hotel for a lunch meeting with Klibi, who had arrived in Baghdad earlier in the day. Aziz, puffing on a large cigar and drinking a glass of whisky, still maintained the tough position he had adopted when he handed the memorandum over to Klibi on July 17.

PIERRE SALINGER WITH ERIC LAURENT

He talked about rising plots against Iraq and said that the United States was part of the plot. "The justice of the Iraqi case is sure," Aziz said. He went on to say that the Royal Family of Kuwait had to go, that they were stealing Iraqi oil and were trying to ruin the Iraqi people.

Klibi had heard that Egyptian President Hosni Mubarak had been telling the Kuwaitis and Americans that Saddam Hussein had told him there would be no invasion of Kuwait. "What did Saddam Hussein tell Mubarak?" Klibi asked.

Aziz puffed on his cigar for a minute. "I don't know what Saddam told Mubarak. What I do know is that everything depends on the Jeddah meeting on July 31 with the Kuwaitis. That meeting will decide everything."

That night, Klibi headed back to Kuwait to report to the Emir.

On July 26, the day intelligence discovered that more than 30,000 Iraqi troops were stationed on the Kuwaiti border, Klibi briefed the Kuwaiti Emir, the Crown Prince, and the Foreign Minister on his meeting in Baghdad. The Kuwaiti leaders were worried but still convinced that an invasion was not going to take place. Klibi mentioned the Jeddah summit on July 31. He was told that the Saudis and the Egyptians would play a role to make sure it succeeded.

What Klibi did not know while he was in these meetings was that that very day the Emir had received an important letter from Saudi Arabia's King Fahd. Welcoming the Emir to the Jeddah summit on July 31, King Fahd wrote to the Emir: "At a time when I am looking forward to this brotherly meeting, may I point out how fully confident I am that your wisdom and foresight will, God willing, achieve our aims, our brother Arabs: to reduce all difficulties and to ensure the love and understanding between the two sisterly states." The Saudi King was obviously telling the Emir that it was important he come to some kind of agreement with Iraq during the summit.

But the Emir had already decided not to go to the summit, which would later anger Saddam Hussein. Instead he wrote a note on King Fahd's letter and passed it on to his brother, Crown Prince Sheikh Saad, whom he would send to Jeddah to represent him.

In the note to his brother the Emir wrote: "We should be present at the meeting under the same previously agreed conditions. It is noteworthy for us to keep in mind our national interests; therefore don't listen to whatever you may hear from the Saudis or Iraqis in regard to brotherhood and maintaining Arab solidarity. Each has his own interests to cater for. The Saudis want to weaken us and to exploit our concessions to the Iraqis so that we will make concessions to them in the demilitarized zone. As for the Iraqis, they wish to compensate for the cost of their war from our resources. Neither demand will bear fruit . . . that is also the position of our friends in Egypt, Washington, and London. We wish you good luck."

The Emir wrote back to King Fahd thanking him for his invitation, telling him he would be represented by his brother and sounding highly optimistic about the Jeddah meeting. "May I also thank and commend your brotherly effort, wisdom and foresight. We have full confidence that our meeting under your guidance and support will, God willing, lead to beneficent results, the reduction of all difficulties and the mutual confidence and love to all."

The exchange of letters and the note to the Crown Prince were already important signals that the Jeddah summit would not work.

On July 27 the CIA sent the White House satellite photographs showing ever greater concentrations of men and equipment on the border. Washington warned Kuwait, Egypt, and Saudi Arabia. But in their replies to the American authorities the Arab leaders dismissed the idea of an invasion and spoke instead of "Iraqi blackmail" designed to acquire two Kuwaiti islands in the Gulf and a disputed oilfield. The State Department and the National Security Council shared this view.

On July 28 the CIA's reports became more specific and more alarming. Saddam had established major supply lines intended for his troops on the border. In particular, a large number of trucks supplying logistical support had been spotted. CIA Director William Webster was convinced that such logistics would not have been necessary if the purpose of the operation were simply intimidation.

New information was reaching the CIA practically hour by hour. Most of it was being collected by the spy satellites of the National Security Agency (NSA).

The NSA, a much bigger and better-budgeted agency than the CIA, is the largest and most advanced information center in the world. Situated in the middle of a forest at Fort Meade, not far from Washington, it is divided into two sections, like the human brain: a right hemisphere with the code name Carillon and a left hemisphere with the code name Lodestone. Its giant computers are capable of processing 150 million to 200 million words a second. Others can handle 320 million words a second, the equivalent of 2,500 books of 300 pages each. Thanks to its listening posts around the world and its spy satellites, the NSA can pick up the most secret conversations and detect the smallest troop movements at any point on the globe. The analysts, mathematicians and decoders of the NSA, all graduates of the best American universities, can even capture details of conversations taking place in a room by measuring electronically the vibrations of the glass in the windows with a small invisible beam.

On July 28 Yasser Arafat met Saddam Hussein in Baghdad. The President asked him to go to Kuwait. "Talk to the Emir and tell him that if he gives me the ten billion dollars I'm asking in return for the use of the Rumailah oil wells on the border, I'll reduce my troops."

Saddam did not specify that he had no intention of invading Kuwait.

King Hussein of Jordan had also seen Saddam Hussein earlier that day. He came out of the meeting convinced that everything now hinged on the Jeddah summit. He had a very uncomfortable feeling that it was the most serious meeting in history between Iraq and Kuwait. Later the same day the King flew to Kuwait and saw the Foreign Minister, Sheikh Sabbah. The minister was rigid: "We cannot bargain over an inch of territory. It's against our constitution. If Saddam comes across the border, let him come. The Americans will get him out."

The King flew back to Amman the next morning and contacted the U.S. and British embassies to relay messages to their countries. His message was clear: "I'm not comfortable about the Jeddah meeting. If it does not progress peacefully, a huge problem will arise."

On July 29 the PLO chief arrived in Kuwait City. He had to wait several hours before the Emir would receive him. Arafat began by setting out the Iraqi proposal. The Emir interrupted curtly: "I don't want to discuss that. In forty-eight hours I'm going to Jeddah for a summit with Iraq. Let's talk instead about the problem of all these Soviet Jews emigrating to Israel."

The Emir's tone was brusque and contemptuous, but although Arafat felt humiliated, he was unable to say anything. Kuwait was one of the main backers of the PLO. At the end of the interview he tried to revert to Saddam's suggestion. The Emir cut him short: "I've already made it quite clear. I don't want to talk about that."

Arafat then met Sheikh Saad, the Crown Prince. This time the conversation was more relaxed.

"You ought to pay the ten billion," said the PLO chief. "The Iraqis are dangerous. As you know, I'm from Kuwait myself. I lived here for several years. Try to resolve this problem."

"I'm going to Jeddah," Prince Saad replied.

"But don't go there empty-handed. Suggest a solution."

The Prince made a tired gesture. "Alas, the final decision is out of our hands." He seemed profoundly worried by the turn events had taken.

"Would you be prepared for a military confrontation?" Arafat asked him.

Saad shook his head. "No, we're not as strong as Iraq. We have no intention of fighting them."

By July 30 the CIA was in a position to assess the state of the Iraqi forces massed near the border with Kuwait: 100,000 men including elite troops of the Republican Guard, 300 tanks, and 300 pieces of heavy artillery. Washington was still silent.

The silence was broken the next day, July 31, when John Kelly entered the Rayburn Building on Capitol Hill to testify before the Middle East subcommittee of the House of Representatives. After his testimony he calmly answered the questions put to him, especially by Representative Lee Hamilton.

"Defense Secretary Richard Cheney has been quoted in the press as saying that the United States was committed to going to the defense of Kuwait if she were attacked. Is that exactly what was said? Could Mr. Kelly clarify this?"

"I don't know the quotation to which you refer, but I have confidence in the administration's position on this matter. We don't have any defense treaty with the Gulf states. That's clear. We support the independence and security of all friendly states in the region. Since the Truman administration, we've maintained naval forces in the area because its stability is in our interests. We call for a peaceful solution to all disputes, and we think that the sovereignty of every state in the Gulf must be respected."

"If, for example, Iraq crossed the Kuwaiti border, for whatever reason, what would our position be regarding the use of American forces?"

"That's the kind of hypothetical question I cannot enter into. Suffice it to say that we would be extremely concerned, but I cannot venture into the realms of hypothesis."

"If such a thing should happen, though, is it correct to say that we have no treaty, no commitment, which would oblige us to use American forces?"

"That's exactly right."

John Kelly's statements were broadcast on the World Service of the BBC and were heard in Baghdad. At a crucial hour, when war and peace hung in the balance, Kelly had sent Saddam Hussein a signal that could be read as a pledge that the United States would not intervene.

In the recent history of American diplomacy there had been only one other example of such a serious miscalculation, and that was Secretary of State Dean Acheson's statement to Congress in 1950 that "South Korea was not part of the United States' zone of defense." Soon afterwards North Korea had invaded the South.

The same day three Iraqi officials left Baghdad for Jeddah, where they were to meet a Kuwaiti delegation and continue the negotiations. This meeting was the last tenuous thread linking the world to a "peace logic." It was a thread that was about to snap. Only three hours before the meeting was due to begin the Emir of Kuwait announced that he himself would not be going and that he would be replaced by the Crown Prince.

To Saddam Hussein the news came as a "deadly insult." He too now decided not to go to Jeddah but to send instead Izzat Ibrahim, number 2 in the Ba'ath Party.

5

"It's Just the Beginning"

The Jeddah conference was a confused and tragic event that resulted in war because nobody was able or willing to avoid it.

The two delegations met in a room in the modern conference center in the Saudi capital at six o'clock in the evening of July 31.

The Kuwaiti delegation included the Prime Minister, Crown Prince Saad, the Foreign Minister and the Justice Minister—the man who had been so clear-sighted in his speech at the cabinet meeting thirteen days earlier.

The Iraqi negotiators—apart from Izzat Ibrahim, vice-president of the Revolutionary Command Council and the number two man in the Ba'ath Party—were Deputy Prime Minister Saddoun Hammadi and Saddam Hussein's cousin, Ali Hassan Al Majid, who a few weeks later would be appointed Governor of Kuwait.

The Kuwaitis and the Iraqis stayed in Jeddah until the next day, August 1, but the real negotiations lasted at most no more than an hour and a half, from six to seven-thirty on the first evening, after which the meeting was adjourned and all the participants went to the mosque to pray.

Crown Prince Abdallah, second in rank and importance in the Saudi kingdom, greeted the two delegations but left the hall as soon as the meeting started. The Iraqis were the first to speak. Izzat Ibrahim read out a prepared speech reiterating, one by one, all the charges against Kuwait. There was no specific threat. Ibrahim read the speech slowly and steadily, without departing from it by a single word. The language was strange, peppered as it was with religious expressions. "It gave us a curious feeling," confided one of the Kuwaitis present at the meeting. "There was something puritanical about it, like a sermon in the mosque."

At first the Kuwaitis were disconcerted by this introduction. Then Crown Prince Saad undertook to calmly refute, one by one, page by page, the grievances that had been set out. The atmosphere was not, as yet, particularly tense, but on both sides it was already beginning to seem likely that the meeting would end in failure.

For Saddoum Hammadi, number two in the Iraqi delegation, "this meeting, on which we had pinned such high hopes, was a great disappointment. We regarded it as perhaps the last chance we had, and we expected the Kuwaitis to come to us with a plan for a solution. We had been in touch with them and had explained everything clearly. But, in fact, they had nothing concrete to offer us, just arguments in their own defense and claims that they hadn't done what we accused them of."

The discussions "were concerned with oil," according to Crown Prince Saad. "The Iraqis also said that the Kuwaitis had begun to establish a police force inside Iraqi territory. They stated that Kuwait had changed its policy and that this new policy endangered the future of the Emirate. I responded to all their remarks and questions in a very direct manner."

At a certain point in the meeting the two main negotiators went into an adjoining room and spoke privately for about ten minutes. Izzat Ibrahim, head of the Iraqi delegation, then asked Prince Saad: "How would you feel if I asked the members of my delegation to come and hear what you have to say?" The Prince accepted. The lack of animosity was in marked contrast to the seriousness of what was at stake.

Things became strained when the discussion moved on to financial matters. Although both the Iraqis and the Kuwaitis later denied that the subject was discussed, it did, in fact, give rise to long and bitter debate. Izzat Ibrahim touched on the demand for $10 billion and added that Iraq would be satisfied with a loan if an outright gift was not possible. After much discussion the Crown Prince agreed, in principle, to a loan of $9 billion. His refusal to grant the extra $1 billion struck the Iraqis as a deliberate attempt to humiliate them. Ibrahim replied: "I don't have authorization from President Saddam Hussein to accept less than $10 billion."

The meeting was adjourned at seven-thirty, and after prayers in the mosque the Kuwaiti delegation returned to the hotel, where they held a meeting while waiting for the dinner to be given by King Fahd. Among those present was Abdullah Bishara, Kuwaiti Secretary of the Gulf Cooperation Council. "We suggested to the Crown Prince that he put forward a proposal that would allow the two sides to agree on four points: first, the ending of all hostile propaganda—the media, especially in Iraq, should put a stop to all their attacks; second, the demobilization of all the forces stationed on the border between the two countries; third—and this was the most important, from a diplomatic point of view—measures designed to nurture mutual confidence, through dialogue, visits, etc.; and, finally, agreement about the next meeting."

It had been decided that the negotiations would continue in Baghdad, a decision that must have confirmed the Kuwaitis in their belief that, for the moment, none of Iraq's threats would be carried out. There was something surreal about the four proposals agreed on by the Kuwaiti delegation, given the urgency of the situation and growing international anxiety.

The world petroleum markets were beginning to react to the massive Iraqi military presence on the Kuwaiti border. That same day, while the two delegations were getting ready to leave for the royal palace where King Fahd was waiting for them, the price of a barrel had risen by 45 cents and Brent Crude was quoted at nearly $20 a barrel.

Dinner was served at nine-thirty. King Fahd, accompanied by King Hussein of Jordan, who had arrived a few hours earlier, had placed Crown Prince Saad on his right and Izzat Ibrahim on his left. Before sitting down to eat, he had been informed of the state of negotiations, in particular the Kuwaiti refusal to improve on an offer of $9 billion.

The atmosphere was heavy. The Saudi monarch tried his best to lighten the mood by talking about the joys of raising and breeding Thoroughbred horses. But the conversation petered out, and King Fahd was left pathetically to conduct a lively monologue. The Iraqis remained silent, and the Kuwaitis seemed both downcast and abstracted. Both sides could barely hide their disappointment, although one of the Kuwaiti negotiators was later to claim that, deep down, the Iraqis must have been feeling pleased: "They were nearing the end of a meeting that had resulted in stalemate. That was exactly what they wanted."

Toward the end of the meal King Fahd turned to his guests with a broad smile and announced that Saudi Arabia would pay the disputed $1 billion, "a gift from my country to Iraq, with no strings attached."

The Iraqis thanked him warmly. Shortly afterward the King rose from the table and went back to his apartments. It was then just after eleven-thirty. The King must have thought that, with his gesture, he had defused the tension between the two delegations, an optimistic assessment shared by King Hussein, who also now rose and left the Kuwaitis and Iraqis alone together.

Crown Prince Saad said to Izzat Ibrahim, "Before we settle the details of the $9 billion loan, there's another question we have to discuss. We must decide on the exact demarcation of our borders. We can do it now, at this meeting, and then the money is yours."

Losing his temper, Ibrahim accused the Kuwaitis of bad faith and asked Saad, "Why wasn't the border dispute brought up when the meeting started?"

The Prince's reply was a strange one: "We had no orders from the Emir to tackle this problem at the beginning of our discussions."

The conversation became more heated. Prince Saad said that Kuwait had received assurances from the British government that Iraq would not attack—no doubt an unfortunate and provocative remark. A little later Izzat Ibrahim told him, "We know perfectly well how to get the money we need from you and the Saudis."

By this time Saad and Ibrahim were standing facing each other, their voices distorted by anger. "Don't threaten us," Saad replied. "Kuwait has very powerful friends [surely a reference to the United States and Britain]. We too have allies. You'll be forced to pay back all the money you owe us."

These threatening words were the last spoken. The two delegations parted unceremoniously and returned to their hotels.

It was just after one-thirty in the morning, and King Fahd had long been asleep.

At ten in the morning on August 1 Saddoum Hammadi was in his hotel room when the telephone rang. The caller was the Deputy Foreign Minister of Kuwait, who suggested that a joint communiqué, approved by both sides, be issued. Hammadi listened carefully to the various points of the suggested text. The one that particularly surprised him was the comment that "progress had been made in the discussions." He replied that he needed to speak first to the leader of his delegation.

He went to Izzat Ibrahim's room and told him of the Kuwaiti move.

"But it's not true!" Ibrahim retorted. "Nothing's been settled. We can't do that."

Hammadi telephoned the Kuwaiti minister and told him that each delegation would issue its own communiqué and would tell the press whatever it wanted.

The Kuwaiti delegation left Jeddah at four in the afternoon. Immediately upon his arrival in Kuwait City, the Crown Prince went to Bayan Palace, a conference center built in 1986, where the Emir had his offices.

Throughout the return flight, he had seemed preoccupied. "I foresee disaster," he had told his colleagues.

Chadli Klibi, the Secretary-General of the Arab League, was in Cairo on the morning of August 1. He had arrived there two days before to participate in an Islamic Conference that would reunite all the Arab nations. When he woke up in the morning he read news dispatches that indicated there had been no accord at the Jeddah summit. Klibi had become confident that the Jeddah meeting would end in an accord, but the news out of the Saudi city concerned him. He picked up the phone and called Sheikh Sabah, the Kuwaiti Foreign Minister. Sheikh Sabah calmed Klibi. He told him that the Jeddah summit was just a protocol meeting and that on August 4 there would be another meeting in Baghdad, where he thought things would be solved. Klibi hung up, feeling that the response was bizarre. He made a second call to Emir Abdallah in Saudi Arabia. Klibi asked him the same question. "What happened yesterday?" The Emir was more direct. "Our Iraqi friends were tough, the Kuwaitis too. But it's just the beginning. Let's wait until Baghdad."

Around noon the same day the Iraqis left Saudi Arabia without even saying good-bye to their host. They took off from Jeddah late in the morning and made a short stop in the holy city of Medina; Deputy Prime Minister Hammadi was a practicing Shi'ite. At four in the afternoon their plane touched down in Baghdad. Ibrahim, the leader of the delegation, immediately went to see Saddam Hussein, who was waiting for him impatiently, and gave him a detailed account of the failure of the meeting. Soon afterward Saddam Hussein summoned the members of the Revolution Command Council. In less than an hour the decision was made to invade Kuwait. The offensive would begin that night.

The same day the price of oil rose another 60 cents. At Abdaly, the only border post open between the two countries, located about 45 miles from Kuwait City, no incidents were reported. Vehicles continued to cross over as usual.

In Israel the press carried the amusing story of a graphologist who had been asked to examine Saddam Hussein's handwriting without being told whose it was. "The man who wrote this," he had said, "needs immediate psychiatric help." Israeli officials did not, as yet, seem particularly worried, nor were they preparing for mobilizaton. That day Major-General Amnon Sha-hak, head of Military Intelligence, got married. At the reception journalists mingling with the guests asked him if there were any risk of military invasion by Iraq. He seemed amused by the question and replied in the negative. A few hours later, he left for his honeymoon.

James Baker arrived in Irkutsk, in the heart of Siberia, at about seven in the evening (local time) for talks with his Soviet opposite number, Eduard Shevardnadze. The two men had no idea that in this charmless city, with its broad avenues lined with gray buildings, they were to be faced with the first real test of the new Soviet–American relationship.

"A new era is beginning," George Bush and Mikhail Gorbachev had declared on many occasions. Neither had foreseen that it would open in such a dramatic manner. Baker was being kept informed of the situation in the Gulf on a special coded line linking him constantly with Washington. His feeling was that things were taking an alarming turn.

He met Shevardnadze at a private dinner. In the five years since he had become Foreign Minister, Shevardnadze, with his white hair and affable smile, had proved a remarkable negotiator. Yet nothing had prepared him for such a post. He had been a KGB officer, Interior Minister, and party boss of the Georgian Republic, where his rule had been highly repressive. The two men took their places in the rear of a black Zil, and the motorcade raced through the streets of Irkutsk. On the avenues American flags waved in the cool wind.

Things were gathering speed. The U.S. government seemed to emerge from its lethargy and take a keen interest in how the situation was developing. A day-long "interagency" meeting, bringing together officials of the main departments concerned, was held at the State Department.

The failure of the Jeddah conference and the size of Iraqi troop concentrations on the border had convinced officials that Saddam Hussein's objective was not merely to put pressure on Kuwait. Those present at the meeting also received information from the CIA that an invasion of Kuwait was imminent.

At the Pentagon, in the middle of the afternoon, the Head of the Joint Chiefs of Staff, General Colin Powell, closeted himself with the army top brass in a room adjoining the military command center. It was a conference room known as "the Tank," the inner sanctum of the U.S. defense system, electronically protected from any possibility of bugging.

Until July 30 the Pentagon had not considered an Iraqi attack likely. According to its analysts, four essential conditions were lacking: a communications system, artillery, munitions, and the logistical means necessary for supporting an offensive. By August 1 all these elements were in place, and still nobody foresaw an invasion. Indeed, one of those present at the meeting, General Norman Schwarzkopf, went straight back to his headquarters in Florida.

Meanwhile in Amman the Jordanian Prime Minister, Mudar Badran, called a closed session of Parliament. Badran had accompanied King Hussein to the Arab capitals on his mission of mediation and only two days before had visited Baghdad and Kuwait. He told the Members of Parliament: "It's clear that Iraq won't compromise on its demands for compensation from Kuwait for the lowering of oil prices. They don't just want their debts annulled. They're still inflexible about the fact that, for them, the overproduction of oil by Kuwait and the Emirates is an act worse than the war with Iran."

For more than three hours Mudar Badran gave the MPs a

detailed review of Iraqi attitudes. "It was clear," one of them was later to say, "that he knew an invasion was going to take place within a few hours and he wanted to prepare us."

By a strange coincidence, Israeli military intelligence learned that an invasion was imminent from Jordanian sources late that afternoon. In accordance with agreements that had been in force for several years, they immediately informed the local CIA station.

In Washington at 6:30 P.M. (10.30 P.M. GMT) Richard Haas, senior director for Middle East Affairs at the National Security Council, left the meeting at the State Department and returned to the White House for a meeting with his chief, General Brent Scowcroft. He gave the general a detailed account of the various statements and viewpoints of those present at the meeting. One thing was clear: there was no longer consensus that Iraq was merely flexing her muscles in order to force Kuwait into negotiating concessions.

Half an hour later Scowcroft and Haas left the offices of the National Security Councils in the basement of the White House and went up to see George Bush in his apartments on the first floor of the main building. The three men talked for forty-five minutes about the results and implications of the "interagency" meeting.

While they were speaking the telephone rang, and Brent Scowcroft took the call. It was Robert Kimmitt, acting Secretary of State in the absence of James Baker and his deputy Lawrence Eagleburger. Kimmitt told Scowcroft that he had just received information, as yet unconfirmed, that the first shots had been fired in Kuwait.

Not long before, Kimmitt had called Baker in Irkutsk, where it was seven in the morning and already August 2. As the line was not a "safe" one—in other words, it was possible that it was bugged—he had to try to convey specific information while keeping his terms vague. Baker got the message: all the signs indicated that an invasion was imminent.

Half an hour later he met Shevardnadze for the second time and told him what he had just heard from Washington. "Our intelligence services," said Baker, "say that the Iraqi forces massed on the Kuwaiti frontier are being continually reinforced. An invasion is anticipated. We hope you can restrain the Iraqis."

The Secretary of State is a friend of George Bush. Both are perfect products of East Coast high society, and both have the gift of expressing the most dramatic facts in a wholly dispassionate way. Baker spoke to Shevardnadze, whom he had grown to respect, in the measured tones that he would use if he were having a conversation with one of his old classmates from Princeton.

The Soviet minister listened to Baker's words with a mixture of incredulity and embarrassment. He replied that the Soviet leaders had known Saddam Hussein for a long time. "He's a client of ours," said Shevardnadze with a smile. "I trust him. I don't think he's planning an invasion."

Soon after that they held a joint press conference, both unaware that Kuwait had already been invaded.

It was about nine o'clock when more detailed information reached President Bush and his two colleagues. It came from the intelligence services and confirmed the scale of the invasion. Saddam Hussein's troops were not just occupying the border areas but sweeping over the whole country.

In Kuwait City Crown Prince Saad was awoken at 1:30 A.M. (10:30 P.M. GMT and 6:30 P.M. in Washington) by an anguished call from the Defense Minister, speaking from army headquarters. The Minister informed him that Iraqi forces had crossed the border. The Prince's first thought was to cling to what he had always believed: that Saddam Hussein wanted to get his hands on the oil wells near the border and perhaps also on the islands of Bubiyan and Warba at the entrance to the Gulf, which he had coveted for years.

Saad immediately contacted several other members of the ruling family. Everybody was stunned, and the news that was gradually reaching army headquarters increased their astonishment. Hundreds of Soviet-made T62 heavy tanks were heading for the capital thirty-five miles away, accompanied by trucks carrying hundreds of men and supply vehicles loaded with petrol and water.

Radio Baghdad broadcast a communiqué that declared that "a group was trying to overthrow the government of Kuwait." Not long afterward a statement by the Revolution Command Council maintained that the attempt had succeeded and that "the young revolutionaries were asking for help from Iraq. In response to the appeal of the new provisional government of Kuwait, Iraq has decided to accept its demand for help." The communiqué went on to specify that Iraq "has been invited to prevent all possibility of foreign intervention in the affairs of Kuwait and the fate of the revolution." Iraqi radio also denounced the Al Sabah family as "traitors and Zionist agents."

The two main Kuwaiti air bases were quickly neutralized. The Ahmad Al Jaber base, near the civil airport, was occupied by parachute units without any Kuwaiti resistance. The Ali Salem base, near the Saudi border, was heavily bombarded before helicopters landed, loaded with men.

British Airways Flight 149 from London to Kuala Lumpur made a stop at Kuwait Airport, eight miles from the capital, just after the invasion began. The Boeing 747 was carrying 367 passengers and eighteen crew members. It touched down at two in the morning. A few minutes later Iraqi planes bombarded the airport, and an armored column advanced toward it. The airport was considered a strategic target. The net had closed in on Flight 149's passengers, who were now potential hostages.

The 25,000 soldiers of the Kuwaiti Army offered little resistance to the massive Iraqi war machine.

By four in the morning it was clear to the Crown Prince and the other members of the Al Sabah family that there was no hope of halting the invasion. They were in constant telephone contact with the U.S. Embassy. When information came in that the first troops were only a few miles from the capital, the Emir and his close relatives decided to leave the Dasman Palace, a luxurious property surrounded by high walls where several members of the ruling family lived. Troops of the Royal Guard began to take up their positions around the palace, but nobody had the slightest hope that they could be an effective defense against Iraqi firepower. Panic was giving way to fear. Orders were followed by counterorders. Should they leave immediately or wait a little longer? Should they call one of the military air bases and ask for a plane to be got ready? The Emir had lost confidence in his air force—and anyway, he added, the Iraqis had probably already neutralized it.

In the brilliantly lit rooms of the palace the Al Sabahs were living, perhaps only temporarily, through the last moments of a monarchy that had lasted two and a half centuries. Thanks to black gold, Kuwait, with a gross national product of nearly $20 billion, had become one of the richest countries in the world. For many years oil had been the source of its wealth; now it was the cause of the country's downfall. Envied by all, blind and unwilling to compromise, Kuwait had not realized that it was a prey ready to be snapped up. And Saddam Hussein was the predator.

The sound of shells startled those in the palace. Exchanges of automatic-weapons fire were getting closer. Through the windows wreaths of black smoke could be seen rising into the sky. Buildings and depots were being directly hit. The Al Sabahs were under no illusion: the Dasman Palace was one of the first objectives—perhaps even the principal target—Saddam Hussein had set his troops. For the Iraqi leader the seizure of Kuwait could certainly not be accomplished without eliminating the members of a despised monarchy.

Several cars were parked in front of the entrance steps, and servants were bustling about ceaselessly, loading them with bags and objects.

At 4:45 A.M. the Al Sabahs settled into their limousines and, for the last time, set off at top speed along the driveways through the magnificent gardens that surrounded the palace. The motorcade tore through the deserted avenues, occasionally passing Kuwaiti armored units heading for a front that was getting ever closer.

All the details had been settled. A last telephone call had been made just before their departure. The cars pulled up outside the U.S. Embassy. The Ambassador was standing at the entrance. He greeted the Emir and his entourage. A few yards away an American army helicopter stood ready to take off. The crew were at the controls, and the blades were already turning. The helicopter could not carry all the fugitives. The Emir, the Crown Prince and a few others got in, and it was decided that the others would travel south to Saudi Arabia by car. The border was only about thirty miles away, and the road was still safe.

The helicopter took off. As it gained height the Emir, exhausted and crushed by what he had been through, pressed his face against the window and watched the first Iraqi columns enter the suburbs of his capital.

Because of the time difference, Japan was the first major industrial and financial power to learn all the details of the invasion. The United States was going to bed; Europe was already asleep; but the Japanese were following the developing situation hour by hour. Lacking raw materials, Japan relied on the Gulf States for 80 per cent of its oil imports. The dramatic events now taking place were considered extremely grave. On the spot market, where freight shipments were negotiated, oil prices soared, and the effect spread like wildfire around the Far Eastern stock markets. The panic felt in these markets would set the tone for the entire stunned world on August 2.

King Hussein was asleep in his palace in the center of Amman when his bedside phone rang. Still dazed, he looked at his alarm clock. It was six in the morning. His ministers and close colleagues had strict, long-standing orders not to disturb him or wake him by phone except in case of emergency.

The voice at the other end of the line was so distorted by excitement that he did not recognize it at first. "Have you heard? Have you heard?" the voice yelled. Hussein realized that his caller was King Fahd. The Saudi King was calling from Jeddah. "Kuwait has been invaded," he said, "and the Iraqis are only a few miles from Kuwait City. You must call Saddam Hussein and ask him to withdraw to the disputed border area."

The King of Jordan tried to calm Fahd, who before placing the call to Amman had desperately tried to reach Saddam Hussein. King Hussein promised to intervene at once.

The Arab League leader, Chadli Klibi, had been sound asleep in Cairo when the war broke out and could not even hear the telephone ringing in the suite at around 4:30 in the morning. His assistant, Chawki Marzouk, was returning from a party at exactly that time and found the telephone in his room ringing also. It was Awadky Abdul Rahman, the Kuwaiti Minister of Planning. "I'm trying to call Klibi, but he's not answering. Please wake him up."

Marzouk asked: "Is it grave?"

Rahman shouted back, "Yes, very grave."

Marzouk rushed up to Klibi's suite and woke him up, putting him through to Rahman. Rahman told him about the invasion. Klibi interrupted: "No, it must just be the takeover of the border areas."

"No, it's the whole of Kuwait, and we need a meeting of the Arab League Foreign Ministers right away."

Klibi hung up and turned to Marzouk. "He's exaggerating. He's trying to scare us." Marzouk told Klibi he believed the information, but when they turned the radio on in the hotel room they got no information.

At around six o'clock Klibi finally got the Saudi Foreign Minister, Prince Faisal. "What a catastrophe," the Prince said. "They are taking over the whole country, undoubtedly the whole country." Now Klibi believed that disaster had struck. He picked up the phone and called the Jordanian Foreign Minister Marwan Al Qasim, who had left Cairo the previous night. Klibi asked Al Qasim to notify King Hussein.

Marwan Al Qasim decided to break the rules and phone the palace, though he was worried about the reception he would get. To his surprise, he discovered that Hussein had already been informed.

At 6:30 P.M. the King phoned Baghdad. He had several numbers on which he could normally contact Saddam Hussein. He tried them all, but in vain. The Iraqi President could not be reached. The King was able to contact only Foreign Minister Tariq Aziz.

Completely unaware of the efforts the King of Jordan was making to speak to him, Saddam Hussein was entrenched in the impressive bunker that he had had constructed near Baghdad. Here, surrounded by the members of the Revolution Command Council and his army chiefs, he was following the progress of his troops inside Kuwait. By 6:30 the invasion was already a success. Saddam's forces were in control of practically the whole country and were beginning to mop up the pockets of resistance that still existed in the capital. Listening to the radio reports coming in from the front, Saddam was unable to hide his satisfaction. The country he had conquered was a fantastic treasure chest. It was also, as far as he was concerned, an integral part of Iraqi territory. But he probably did not realize that, in correcting what he saw as an injustice committed by the colonial powers, he had issued a challenge to the rest of the world.

In Washington it was 11.30 P.M. on August 1. At about nine, directly after their meeting with George Bush, Brent Scowcroft and Richard Haas had gone to the Situation Room, a specially equipped conference room in the basement of the White House. It was surrounded by several rooms whose walls were covered with huge maps showing the different regions of the world. The information passed on to the White House every morning by the intelligence services was reproduced on these maps. The Situation Room was fitted with extremely sophisticated computer equipment, which allowed those in the room to be linked instantaneously with any spot on the globe.

A scrambled video link was immediately established between

the White House, the Pentagon, the State Department, the CIA, and the headquarters of the Chiefs of Staff. Besides Scowcroft and Haas, those taking part were Deputy Treasury Secretary John Robson, Robert Kimmitt, acting for James Baker, CIA Director William Webster and his deputy Dick Kerr, Admiral Dave Jeremiah, deputy head of the Joint Chiefs of Staff, and Deputy Defense Secretary Paul Wolfowitz.

Thanks to the video link, these men were able to talk and to exchange and compare information without leaving their offices. They quickly confirmed the scale of the invasion. Brent Scowcroft coordinated the various contributions, stamping his own level-headedness and precision on the meeting.

He regularly left the room to phone George Bush, who had stayed in his apartments. At eleven they had a final conversation before the President went to bed.

Several measures were agreed upon, including the convening of an emergency meeting of the National Security Council at eight the following morning. It was also decided that all Iraqi assets, and certainly all Kuwaiti assets, must be frozen before the invading powers could seize them. To be fully effective, such a move had to be coordinated worldwide and immediately.

For several years the Kuwaiti authorities had been allocating 10 per cent of the country's oil revenues to two causes: by an irony of history, 2 percent had been devoted to loans to Iraq during the war with Iran, and the other 8 percent had been transferred to a "fund for future generations" managed by the Kuwait Investment Office, a giant holding company based in London. According to estimates, the total value of the portfolio of investments managed by the KIO was on the order of $100 billion to $120 billion. Kuwaiti investments in the United States accounted for more than 10 percent of all foreign investments. The Emirate had invested in America between $25 billion and $30 billion in the form of shares, Treasury bonds and real estate.

In Spain Kuwait was the largest foreign investor, and Kuwaitis sat on the boards of several major companies, including some in fields as sensitive as the press, defense and hydrocarbons. In London the KIO played a vital role in the economic and business life of Great Britain, holding large numbers of shares, especially in banking and hotel chains. For a short time the KIO had even held as much as 22 percent of the shares of British Petroleum, but because of the hostile reaction of the British government it had reduced its interest to 9.9 percent. In Germany the KIO was a shareholder in many major firms, such as Daimler-Benz and Hoechst. In Japan too the Emirate was the largest foreign investor in both Treasury bonds and stock-market shares. All the main capitalist countries, including South Africa, had been penetrated by the KIO and its financial holdings.

In just a few hours Saddam Hussein had changed the balance of power. By seizing the Kuwaiti oilfields he had gained control of more than a fifth of the oil produced in the world. In addition, the Emirate's investments could provide Saddam with a huge source of funds for his military ambitions and an extra means of applying pressure on the economies of the West.

To counter this danger, U.S. officials acted quickly. A number of officials living in Washington and its suburbs were woken in the middle of the night and summoned to the White House. All of them were lawyers working for the Justice Department. The summons had been succinctly phrased, and none of them knew, as they presented themselves to the security officers at the entrance to the White House, exactly why they had been called. In a few minutes the purpose was explained: they were to produce, as quickly as possible, a legal document to be signed by the President that would allow for the freeze of all Iraqi and Kuwaiti assets on U.S. territory. It was a move hostile to Baghdad but designed to safeguard the interests of the Kuwaiti government now in exile.

While they were at work Deputy Treasury Secretary John Robson was telephoning the governors of the central banks in all the European and Asian capitals. Most of them, surprised by a call so early in the morning, learned of the invasion from Robson. His task was to ask them to apply identical measures as soon as possible in order to freeze all assets before Baghdad, through its intermediaries now in control in Kuwait City, took the initiative.

George Bush was awoken at 4:45 A.M. The documents were ready. He appended his signature. The assets were now effectively frozen. A communiqué announcing the move was drawn up in the White House Press Office.

While President Bush signed the documents he turned to the head of the National Security Council, General Brent Scowcroft, who had brought them up. "Make sure the State Department starts contacting the Arab nations to make sure they join in condemning the Iraqis' invasion of Kuwait." Scowcroft said he would deal with the situation immediately.

There had been time, during the all-night session in the Situation Room, to decide on a further step. Once the initial astonishment had passed—nobody had really believed Saddam Hussein's threats—those present in the room, or linked to it by video, had begun to lay the foundations of a response.

The military option had not yet been discussed, but the diplomatic choices were clearer. The Emir and his colleagues, now refugees in Saudi Arabia, were contacted as soon as they arrived in Jeddah. American officials worked closely with them to arrange an emergency session of the United Nations Security Council.

At the United Nations headquarters in Manhattan there was an unusual amount of activity for such an early hour. Cars were arriving constantly, bringing Ambassadors and their delegations. At 4:00 A.M. the first resolution on the Iraqi crisis, Resolution 660, was passed. It called for Iraq's immediate and unconditional withdrawal from Kuwait and the restoration of the *status quo ante*. Only Yemen abstained, while the USSR, China, and even Cuba voted with the United States, France, and Great Britain. The Iraqi Ambassador at the UN responded by stating that his government had answered a call for help from "young Kuwaiti revolutionaries."

The resolution also called for Iraq and Kuwait "to begin immediately intensive negotiations for the resolution of their differences and supports all efforts in this regard, and especially those of the Arab League."

In Washington Brent Scowcroft, Richard Haas, and all those who had taken part in the all-night marathon, which had lasted from nine in the evening to five in the morning, knew that they had only three hours to return home, take a bath, and change. The National Security Council meeting in the White House with George Bush was scheduled to begin at eight o'clock precisely.

In Irkutsk at 10:30 A.M. (9:30 the previous evening in Washington), after their press conference, the U.S. Secretary of State and the Soviet Foreign Minister left for the airport. Shevardnadze was returning to Moscow, and Baker was flying to the Mongolian capital, Ulan Bator. His colleague, Dennis Ross, was to go to Moscow in Shevardnadze's plane.

During his flight Baker received a call from Washington on his special line and was informed in detail about the Iraqi invasion. While his plane was flying toward Mongolia—that buffer state with a population of 2 million, dozing between the USSR and China, apparently so removed from the madness and panic that had seized the rest of the world—Baker went to the rear of the plane, where the press were sitting, and told them the news.

An hour later Shevardnadze landed in Moscow. He still had no idea what was happening. Hardly had he disembarked than a journalist from the Tass news agency rushed toward him. "What's your comment on the invasion?"

"What invasion?" asked Shevardnadze, taken aback.

"Why, Iraq's invasion of Kuwait!"

In confusion, the Minister refused to answer questions. "I haven't been informed. I'm going to consult my advisers." He turned abruptly to his colleague, Sergei Tarasenko, and said angrily, "Find out what's going on at once."

As for Ross, he went immediately to the U.S. Embassy and contacted Baker. He suggested that it would be a good idea to issue a Soviet–American communiqué that would not only condemn the invasion but also call for concerted action against Iraq. Baker approved of the idea and phoned George Bush to get his agreement. The President considered the idea an excellent one and gave him the go-ahead. Baker called Ross in Moscow and said, "Draft the text, but make sure it's a good communiqué."

It was agreed that Baker would cut short his trip to Mongolia and fly to Moscow, where he would deliver the joint communiqué with Eduard Shevardnadze. Ross was given the task of negotiating this matter with the Soviets. He spoke to Sergei Tarasenko, telling him that such a move would dissuade other Arab countries from siding with Iraq and would dash Saddam Hussein's hopes of playing on the rivalry between the superpowers, as he had in the past. At first Tarasenko seemed hesitant, then, after consulting Shevardnadze, he told Ross, "We agree."

"Good," Baker's colleague replied, "but the text will have to be a strong one. Don't forget that the Secretary of State will be coming to Moscow especially to read it."

Abu Iyad, the number-two man in the PLO, in charge particularly of security and intelligence matters, was asleep in his villa in the suburbs of Tunis. His wife, who usually lived in Kuwait City, had just arrived. They were awoken by a phone call from members of their family in the Kuwaiti capital who told them that fighting was taking place not far from their house. Abu Iyad dressed and went at once to see Yasser Arafat, who was in the habit of working late into the night in his hosue in the Samed district. The PLO chief knew all about the situation. He too had been informed by family members who lived in Kuwait City. The two men decided to visit several Arab capitals the next day.

6

"Will You Leave
Kuwait?"

It was just after midnight in London (2 A.M. in the Gulf) when
the Foreign Secretary, Douglas Hurd, received a phone call
from the British Embassy in Kuwait informing him of the invasion. He noted down the details, then walked along the deserted corridors of the Ministry and, on a special line, phoned
the twenty-four-hour information-gathering service at 10 Down-
ing Street. Margaret Thatcher, the Prime Minister, was contacted immediately. She had just arrived in Aspen, Colorado,
where she was due to take part in a conference with George
Bush the next day. It was then seven in the evening in Aspen
and, thanks to the time difference, still August 1.

The Japanese Prime Minister, Kaifu, was taking a five-day vacation at Guma, a mountain resort some 50 miles north of
Tokyo. He was informed of the invasion by Foreign Ministry
officials an hour after it was launched. It was then seven in the

morning on August 2. Kaifu's first reaction was: "How regrettable."

Ambassador April Glaspie, who had emerged so full of confidence from her interview with Saddam Hussein just a few days earlier, was stunned. She learned of the invasion on the morning of August 2 when she switched on the television in her hotel room in London, where she was staying with her mother. Her dog, which had remained behind in Baghdad, would soon be evacuated on one of the first flights carrying American women.

Germany's Chancellor, Helmut Kohl, was staying at Saint Gilgen in Austria, in a villa by a lake that he rented every year for his summer vacation. At 9 A.M. his personal assistant, Eduard Ackermann, called him from Bonn to tell him the news. Kohl was not to receive any message from a Western political leader until George Bush phoned him three days later to advise him of his decision to send troops to Saudi Arabia.

In Kuwait City there was panic. Many inhabitants tried to escape to Saudi Arabia, but the roads had already been cut off and were under the control of Iraqi troops. Families were stopped at roadblocks and forced out of their vehicles, and car phones—common pieces of equipment—were torn out to prevent them from being used to transmit details of troop positions.

Helicopters were flying over the city, and 300 tanks were patrolling the deserted avenues. Vehicles were burning, and mortar and automatic-weapons fire could be heard in the financial district and near the Emir's palace, which was surrounded by fifty heavy tanks. It was in this fighting, the fiercest of the whole invasion, that the Emir's youngest brother, Sheikh Fahd, the head of the Kuwait Olympic Committee who had stayed behind, would be killed. A few Iraqi escort vessels would be destroyed by Kuwaiti patrol boats equipped with missiles, but all in all there would be only a few pockets of resistance to the Iraqi army. By mid-afternoon the firing had practically ceased. More than 200 Kuwaitis had been killed.

In a few hours Saddam Hussein had realized his dream. He now controlled 20 per cent of the world's oil reserves and over 100 miles of coastline giving him direct access to the Persian Gulf.

Stunned by what had happened, the rest of the Arab world was discovering how determined Saddam Hussein really was. No country close to Iraq would be able to feel safe: Jordan was under threat as well as Iraq's brother and enemy, Syria, and above all the wealthy and vulnerable Saudi Arabia, which was now in the front line. The Iraqi leader had the military means to go much farther in his conquests. From the suburbs of Kuwait City came a clandestine radio message: "Oh, Arabs, the blood and honor of Kuwait have been violated; come to her aid." The voice uttering these words added, tearfully: "The children, the women and the old men of Kuwait are appealing to you for help."

But the Arab world had been struck dumb and made no response to this call for help, partly out of fear but mainly because the reaction everywhere was confusion, even chaos.

From August 2 onward, King Hussein would make intense efforts to prevent the situation from escalating.

It was almost seven hours after his first call to Saddam Hussein that the Iraqi leader called King Hussein at 1 P.M. Saddam seemed neither tense nor intransigent. "We had to go in. I am now in full control of Kuwait. We were driven to that. I am committed to withdrawal from Kuwait. It will start within days and will last several weeks. Please do whatever you can with the Arabs to persuade them that condemnations and threats don't work with us. We may end up with Kuwait being part of Iraq. It is very important that they not give cover to external involvement." The King said it was necessary for the two of them to meet. They agreed that the King would fly to Baghdad either that night or early the next morning.

The King emerged from this conversation confirmed in his belief that a quick negotiated settlement was possible within an Arab framework. He immediately phoned the Egyptian President, Hosni Mubarak, who was leaving for Alexandria, and told him of his talk with the Iraqi leader and of his plan to call an Arab mini-summit, either in Cairo or in Riyadh, for the morning of August 4. Until then, the King insisted, the Arab countries should avoid any statement hostile to Iraq so that the summit would not be jeopardized. "I'll support you," said Mubarak. They agreed that the King would come through Alexandria on his way to Iraq in order to discuss these plans with the Egyptian President in greater detail. Before ringing off, he suggested that Mubarak talk to Saddam Hussein. "No," came the reply. "He's disappointed me."

In Cairo, at 9 A.M., ministers of Arab states started to gather in a salon in the Hotel Semramis. Chadli Klibi had become convinced a meeting was necessary and had called the Egyptian Foreign Ministry, which delegated two men to him to help notify all of the key players. Klibi also called Dusama Zhaoui, the sub-minister of Iraqi Affairs, who was representing his country at the Islamic conference. He told him an Arab League meeting was starting at nine. Zhaoui protested. "Why call a meeting so urgently? Why don't you wait until my government decides what to do?" Klibi refused, saying the meeting was vital. But the ministers arrived slowly, and the meeting did not actually start until 12:15 P.M.

By the time the session opened, in an atmosphere of tension and confusion, the invasion was more than ten hours old and the Iraqi army was in complete control of Kuwait.

Farouk Kaddoumi, Foreign Minister of the PLO, presided over the debate, in accordance with a rotation system that called for each meeting of the League's Council to be chaired by a different Foreign Minister.

The Kuwaiti delegation demanded the immediate implementation of the Arab defense pact that called on all Arab nations to act in defense of a member country that had been attacked. With the exception of the United Arab Emirates, however, the ministers present preferred, by a large majority, to adopt a wait-and-see policy.

The Syrian Foreign Minister, Farouk Al Shara, made a surprising speech in which he stated that his country's relations with Kuwait were bad (again due to non-payment of money) but that relations with Iraq had been getting better. Nevertheless, he added, "Syria abides by the Charter of the Arab League, which considers the invasion of one Arab country by another an illegal act."

The Saudi Foreign Minister, Prince Faisal, also gave a surprising speech. He talked about the special rotations that existed between Saudi Arabia and Iraq and went on to say that warm friendship existed between his leader, King Fahd, and Saddam Hussein. "Saudi Arabia is not in accord with the invasion of Kuwait, but we are persuaded that Saddam Hussein will pull out."

Chadli Klibi, the leader of the Arab League, had persuaded Dusama Zhaoui, the sub-minister of Iraqi Affairs, to attend the meeting, but he refused to answer questions posed to him by different foreign ministers. "I'm not here to talk," he said. "You have to wait until my delegation arrives." He announced that the delegation would be headed by the Deputy Prime Minister, Saddoum Hammadi, and that he would arrive early in the evening with a large delegation. At 2 P.M. the meeting was adjourned, and it was agreed that it would resume at 6 P.M. There was great impatience to hear the message that everyone was sure that Hammadi would be bearing.

The White House, 8 A.M., August 2. As the session of the Arab League was being adjourned in Cairo, George Bush entered the Cabinet Room adjoining the Oval Office. All those summoned to the meeting had already taken their seats around the huge table that took up most of the room: Vice President Dan Quayle; White House General Secretary John Sununu; Treasury Secretary Nicholas Brady; Attorney General Richard Thornburgh; Defense Secretary Richard Cheney; CIA Director William Webster; Chairman of the Joint Chiefs of Staff Colin Powell; General Schwarzkopf, head of CENTCOM (U.S. Central Command), who a few days later would be put in charge of the American expeditionary force in Saudi Arabia; General Brent Scowcroft; his deputy, Richard Haas; and Robert Kimmitt. All the key people in the Bush Administration were there to face the greatest crisis since they had entered office.

Journalists accredited to the White House were allowed to enter the room for a few moments, and Bush made his first public statement on the crisis: "Let me tell you that the United States strongly condemns the invasion and calls for an immediate withdrawal. There is no place for this kind of brutal aggression in today's world."

Then the doors were closed again for a top-secret meeting that lasted more than an hour.

The discussion concentrated to a large extent on retaliatory measures, both diplomatic and economic, to be taken against Iraq. When the meeting began White House General Secretary John Sununu, a well-built man with a reputation as an authoritarian, turned to Defense Secretary Cheney and suggested "sending B2s [planes that can escape radar detection] to bomb Iraq." Nobody knew whether he was serious.

Cheney seemed embarrassed. He paused for a moment and then replied: "We have only one plane of that type. The others haven't been tested sufficiently to be considered ready for combat."

In point of fact, the Bush Administration was faced with a problem of strategic doctrine. Military intervention in the Gulf had been considered a possibility for ten years. After the fall of the Shah of Iran in 1979, President Jimmy Carter had created a rapid-deployment force whose principal mission would be to protect the region's oilfields. A secret plan, with the code number 90-1002, had been drawn up at that time. Unfortunately, two things that the plan had not taken into account were Iraqi aggression and the loss of Kuwait. The purpose of the plan had been simply to prepare for a confrontation with the Soviet Union in the Gulf region.

Responsibility for putting this plan into operation fell to CENTCOM, the military command center created in 1983. But, despite the $2,000 billion spent over the past eight years to modernize and strengthen the armed forces, the military authorities were in a difficult position. Their troops had been trained for combat in theaters of operations such as Europe or Korea, not for a war in the desert. Moreover, the Pentagon had been caught short. It had had several months to prepare Operation Just Cause, which had led to the sending of troops to Panama to capture General Noriega; now, as one of those present at the meeting would later confide, "We were back at square one."

That point became obvious when George Bush asked what troops were immediately available. The reply was categorical:

2,500 men of the 82nd Airborne Division, based at Fort Bragg, North Carolina, could be sent at once, but the dispatch of larger contingents would take at least four weeks. Even then, the balance of forces would still be highly unfavorable to the Americans, given the 1 million men and 5,500 tanks at Saddam Hussein's disposal. As one of the military chiefs present at the White House meeting put it, bluntly, "There is no satisfactory military option. We just don't have the guys on the ground." Indeed, despite repeated efforts by Washington, Saudi Arabia had always rejected the idea of U.S. bases on its territory.

It was now 9 A.M. George Bush ordered that all the conceivable miltiary options be presented to him by Saturday, 4 August—the day after next—at his summer residence at Camp David. A possible trip to Saudi Arabia by Defense Secretary Cheney was also discussed, but no definite decision was reached.

At 9:15, Bush left the meeting and returned to the Oval office to pick up a few files. Then he proceeded quickly to the south lawn of the White House. A helicopter was waiting there to take him to the Andrews Air Force base, where the presidential Boeing, Air Force One, was ready for take-off. Bush was to go to Aspen, Colorado, to deliver a speech on defense matters. Although the engagement had been scheduled months before, because of the deepening crisis he had considered cancelling it. But at the last moment he decided to go ahead because he was due to meet British Prime Minister Margaret Thatcher. She was to exercise considerable influence on the President. During the flight, with the help of Brent Scowcroft, Bush emended the text of his speech, linking the Gulf crisis with the need for the United States to maintain appropriate means of defense. When the alterations had been made, he gave orders to call Hosni Mubarak's residence in Alexandria.

Half an hour earlier King Hussein had landed in the Egyptian coastal city at the controls of his own plane. It was 4 P.M. in Egypt. He began his discussion with the Egyptian President by restating his firm belief that the problem could be resolved and that Saddam Hussein could be persuaded to leave Kuwait, on condition that he was not condemned by the Arab League. But the King made it absolutely clear that there should be no verbal attack on Iraq before the summit scheduled for August 4 had taken place. Mubarak agreed.

While the two men were talking, they decided it was important to have a conversation with President Bush. They put in a call through the White House and reached the President as he was flying at an altitude of 37,000 feet between Washington, DC, and Aspen, Colorado. The President's voice was audible. The King outlined his phone conversation with Saddam Hussein and his plan to go to Baghdad. He said it was essential that an Arab solution be achieved immediately. He urged President Bush not to put pressure on Arab states to issue communiqués criticizing Iraq for its invasion of Kuwait for at least forty-eight hours to give him the time to put together a solution. "We can settle the crisis, George," the King said. "We can deal with it. We just need a little time."

"You've got it," Bush replied. "I'll leave it to you."

The drawing room where the two leaders were speaking opened onto a wide terrace overlooking the sea. Alexandria, a slow, lazy city conducive to peace and optimism, rose in the distance. His brief stopover seemed to fill King Hussein with the certainty that the Kuwait conflict was a miscalculation that would soon be forgotten. Mubarak was more skeptical, but made the effort—or pretended—to believe the same thing.

Jerusalem, 5:00 P.M. An emergency session devoted to Iraq was just beginning in the Israeli Parliament, the Knesset. Not long before, Defense Minister Moshe Arens had received the American Ambassador and had offered to supply the United States with all the help it needed with regard to intelligence.

In fact, the Iraqi attack had brought to light a certain number of Israeli shortcomings. Iraq was not a country "well covered" by the Israeli secret service, which was faced with a problem of recruitment, as well as the fact that it had no spy satellites in that region.

Since 1981 the Americans had been refusing to hand over to Israel any photographs of information obtained by spy satellites beyond an area of 30 miles around the Jewish state. Washington considered this distance "a security zone sufficient to avoid all immediate danger." The measure had been taken not long after the Israelis had bombed the Iraqi nuclear plant at Osiraq.

There had been a meeting of the Israeli cabinet at 8:30 that morning. The atmosphere had been tense. Some of the ministers, including Ariel Sharon, had been highly critical of these weaknesses, and a statement by Brigadier-General Danny Rothschild, deputy head of Military Intelligence (his chief was still on his honeymoon) had given rise to fierce debate. The feeling of most Israeli officials was that the special services had been caught off guard, not only by the timing of the invasion but also by its scale.

While the American aircraft carrier *Independence* and six escort vessels were on their way to the Gulf, to be joined by a cruiser, a destroyer and five frigates, Lloyd's of London announced the immediate introduction of a war premium payable by all ships operating in that area. And London's brokers watched the price of North Sea oil rise to $24 a barrel.

Before leaving Amman King Hussein had tried unsuccessfully to contact King Fahd. He had then given orders to his Foreign Minister, Marwan Al Qasim, to arrange a meeting with the Saudi monarch and to fly to Jeddah. After several attempts and a long wait, the Saudi reply reached the Minister: "Don't come."

Hosni Mubarak, though, was luckier. It was now 6:00 P.M. and King Hussein, who had just left to fly to Baghdad, had asked him to phone several Arab leaders, including King Fahd, to ask them to remain calm and not to take sides for the next forty-eight hours. Mubarak passed on Hussein's request to the Saudi monarch, who agreed.

Meanwhile in Cairo the delegates of the member States of the Arab League were gathering in the Hotel Semiramis. The Iraqi delegation was expected to arrive, but the wait proved a long one. The representatives of the Gulf states were furious at the League's refusal to condemn the invasion. They were joined by the Syrians, sworn enemies of Iraq. For three and a half hours, in an atmosphere of increasing tension, the delegates waited for the Iraqis to arrive. It was 9:30 P.M. when Saddoum Hammadi finally walked up the center aisle to the podium.

Hammadi unfolded a document that the delegates expected to be a peace plan, but they were to be bitterly disappointed. He began by stating, "The situation in Kuwait is not negotiable." Hammadi had no proposal to make. For half an hour he merely repeated the familiar Iraqi case like a litany: certain Arab nations and the United States had entered into an economic conspiracy against Iraq by maintaining oil prices at a very low level and by preventing Baghdad from stabilizing an economy that had been severely damaged by the Iran–Iraq War. Hammadi's speech lacked the slightest hint of concession. He stated firmly once again that it was Iraq that had prevented

Iran from overrunning the region. During all those years of war, he said, "Iraq acted as a shield for all the Gulf states. Despite this protection those states later refused to give us the financial aid we desperately needed."

Hammadi returned to his seat. The audience was stunned. Baghdad seemed to be closing the door to all compromise. Suddenly the Kuwait crisis had taken on a more somber complexion. Earlier optimism had given way to abject depression.

By the time the meeting was adjourned, to be resumed at nine the following morning, the delegates were no longer under any illusions as to the outcome of the discussions. The only hope for an Arab solution now rested on the meeting between Saddam Hussein and the King of Jordan.

The King had stayed in Alexandria late in the evening, hoping that he could make a stop in Saudi Arabia to see King Fahd before flying to Baghdad. But the Saudis had turned down his offer, so he returned to Amman, slept for a few hours and headed to Baghdad early on the morning of August 3. Before leaving for Baghdad King Hussein made another call to President Mubarak. "Are we on track?" the King asked the Egyptian President. Mubarak answered that Kuwait would probably not attend the mini-summit but that it would include Egypt, Saudi Arabia, Jordan, Yemen, and Iraq.

Just before his plane landed in Aspen, Bush contacted James Baker, who was getting ready to leave Mongolia. "Jim," he said, "that joint statement must show a very high level of collaboration between the Soviet Union and us, otherwise there's no point in your going to Moscow."

As soon as he arrived the President had his first meeting with Margaret Thatcher. With the inevitable handbag under her arm, she clasped his hand. Her first words were: "You must know,

George, he's not going to stop." That, increasingly, was a fear that Bush shared. While the conference on defense matters continued a few yards away, he phoned President Salehih of Yemen, one of Iraq's few allies. The mountains of Colorado rose nearby, giving the occasion the atmosphere of a university summer school.

After delivering his speech Bush called King Fahd's residence in Saudi Arabia and reiterated the absolute determination of the United States to defend his kingdom. Fahd thanked him profusely, but Bush's solicitude seemed to embarrass rather than cheer him. A shy man of delicate health, Fahd gave the impression of being out of his depth. As he had feared, Saudi Arabia was now in the front line. Since its creation, sixty-three years earlier, the kingdom had been an island of stability, but the invasion of Kuwait was an event he described as "tragic." The Emir and his family were now his guests. In a strange way, history had come full circle. Eighty-eight years earlier, in 1902, Ibn Seoud, the founder of the kingdom, who was then a fugitive, had found shelter in Kuwait with the Al Sabahs.

Before he returned to Washington, George Bush and Margaret Thatcher closeted themselves in the Catto residence, a luxury chalet belonging to the U.S. Ambassador to Great Britain. Thatcher advised the President to take the firmest possible stand and to mobilize the whole world under the auspices of the United Nations. The military options were not discussed, but, according to an eyewitness, "she spoke of Saddam Hussein rather as one of her predecessors, Anthony Eden, had spoken of Gamal Abdel Nasser during the Suez crisis, comparing him with Hitler."

By 4:00 P.M., when the presidential plane left Aspen for Washington, the Pentagon had already taken a certain number of measures. Crews of the giant C141 cargo aircraft had been urgently summoned. All leaves had been canceled, and all crew members had been given three hours to return to their bases. Astonished, the men left their families and friends abruptly, completely unaware of the reason for their recall. By early evening they were flying over the Atlantic. Twenty-eight C141 crews were landed at the American base at Rhein Main in West Germany and a further twenty-six at Torrejon in Spain. They were the first link in the giant aerial chain that would be forged with Saudi Arabia within a few days.

A big dance taking place in a mess hall was suddenly interrupted by an officer's announcement that all the men present should report for duty immediately. There was no further explanation. They were not to return. They were members of special operations units whose job was to take part in dangerous missions such as commando raids or a response to the taking of hostages. That very night they would be sent to the Middle East.

Cairo, 8:00 A.M., August 3. Delegates due to take part in the meeting of the Arab League scheduled for nine o'clock were informed that the session had been postponed until six that evening. Nothing could be said or decided until the outcome of the meeting between Saddam Hussein and the King of Jordan was known. The eyes of the whole Arab world were on Baghdad.

A radio message from occupied Kuwait launched a desperate appeal: "What has happened to the agreements reached among Arab states, the agreements reached among the states of the Gulf, the agreements reached among the Islamic nations? Oh brothers in language and blood, Arabism and Islam have grown with us. Kuwait is calling for your help."

Kuwaitis stranded in Cairo by the invasion came out onto

the streets in tears. An Egyptian officer told one of them: "This situation is a disgrace to the Arab world. We're sitting here watching, as if nothing had happened."

Arabs reading their newspapers were incredulous. Not a single one denounced the Iraqi invasion of Kuwait. The editors had received strict orders from their leaders to remain neutral. The only Arab country whose press openly supported Saddam Hussein was Jordan.

At 9:30 A.M. King Hussein arrived in Baghdad and was received immediately by Saddam in the presidential palace. The meeting would last several hours but would end in agreement. The King asked several specific questions of the Iraqi leader.

"Are you going to the mini-summit planned for tomorrow?"

Saddam Hussein nodded. "I'll be there."

"Will you leave Kuwait?"

"Yes, if my differences with the Emirate can be settled." Later in the conversation, he specified: "I don't want any members of the Al Sabah family to attend the summit. I would prefer to negotiate an agreement with King Fahd. I've always had better relations with him."

The Iraqi President gave his guest the impression of a benevolent leader prepared to make major compromises. His one moment of anger was when the King mentioned the Arab League's threats to condemn him. "Let's not scratch our eyes out," Saddam replied. "If things move in that direction, I'll just say that Kuwait is part of Iraq and annex it." Then he leaned toward the King and lowered his voice, as if about to impart a secret. "And anyway . . ." He paused for a moment, as if to give his statement more weight. "I've signed a non-aggression pact with Saudi Arabia."

When the two men parted they embraced warmly and the

King had an optimistic smile on his face, convinced that he had managed to deal with the crisis. A few hours later Saddam Hussein issued a communiqué announcing that he would begin to withdraw his troops from Kuwait on Sunday, August 5, but that there was no question of restoring the royal family.

As King Hussein was leaving Baghdad to return to Amman, PLO chief Yasser Arafat was arriving in Tripoli from Tunis. He would later be going to Egypt, Iraq, and Saudi Arabia on a parallel mission of mediation. There was a large Palestinian population in Kuwait, occupying positions of responsibility, and the sums it donated to the PLO made up a large part of that organization's budget.

In Tripoli Arafat found Gaddafi deeply disturbed by the invasion. "Abu," he insisted [Abu is the PLO chief's real name], "it's absolutely essential to find a peaceful solution. I've drawn up a two-point plan." He snatched up a piece of paper from the table in front of him. Arafat, dressed in uniform, with the inevitable *keffieh* on his head, listened and smiled benevolently. For many years relations between Gaddafi and the Palestinians had been complex and, occasionally, unpredictable. "First," Gaddafi continued, "Iraq must withdraw to the disputed border areas. Then a member of the Kuwaiti royal family—not the Emir—will return to Kuwait, and the people themselves will be able to choose their ruler."

The second point of the proposal was quite unrealistic, but Arafat made no comment.

That day, August 3, would, in fact, see control of the crisis gradually slip out of Arab hands.

At the White House, late that afternoon, Bush opened the meeting of the National Security Council. With him were Defense Secretary Richard Cheney, Brent Scowcroft, head of the NSC, his deputy Richard Haas, and Chairman of the Joint Chiefs of Staff Colin Powell.

General Powell confirmed to the President that all the military options were currently being studied and would be presented to him the following day, as planned. Powell, fifty-three years of age, was a Vietnam veteran who had already been involved in five crises, including the invasion of Panama and the landing of Marines in Liberia to evacuate American nationals. "There's no legitimate use of military force," he liked to say, "without a political objective." It was a point of view with which Bush could not help but agree.

The members of the Executive seated around the table had at their disposal a number of pieces that fit the Gulf jigsaw puzzle, including the support of the UN and NATO. What they lacked was a range of military choices and the support of the Arab world.

Questioned by George Bush about the risks that would be incurred by the first American troops sent into the field, Powell replied without hesitation: "The risks are enormous. Our forces would be extremely vulnerable to Iraqi attack. If you finally decide to commit military forces, Mr. President, it must be done as massively and decisively as possible. Choose your target, decide on your objective, and try to crush it."

Bush nodded but made no comment.

The meeting ended two hours later, and while his colleagues went off to stretch their legs he telephoned King Fahd again and tried to convince him that, according to the information he had at his disposal, Saddam Hussein was about to march on Saudi Arabia.

King Fahd demurred, saying that he still had confidence in King Hussein's efforts to reach a negotiated settlement and to persuade the Iraqi President to withdraw from Kuwait. He reminded Bush that an Arab mini-summit was due to be held the following day, August 4.

"But if things got worse, Your Majesty, would you accept American military aid?"

The King did not reply. The silence lasted so long that Bush, sure that Fahd had not heard the question because of a problem on the line, repeated it.

"If things get worse," the King finally answered, in a resigned tone, "yes, we'll accept."

There was another factor in the crisis that exasperated George Bush, and that was that he had been misled. He had long been a firm believer in the importance of personal ties between leaders. One of his closest colleagues describes him as "conducting a form of personal diplomacy," in particular by often telephoning heads of state for informal chats. "George," says a friend, "likes to be known as 'Dear old George,' appreciated by everyone for his warmth." But in the Kuwait affair, in spite of the ever more specific and alarming reports that had been reaching him through the intelligence agencies, the President had believed, right until the last moment, that Iraq would not invade, simply because two leaders he had trusted, King Hussein of Jordan and President Hosni Mubarak of Egypt, had constantly assured him of this. Bush had considered them a more reliable source of information than all the secret reports and all the satellite photos that arrived hourly on his desk.

The Bush Administration had, in fact, committed the same error of judgment that the Israeli leaders made before the outbreak of the Yom Kippur War in 1973. In both cases the special services had possessed all the information necessary to elucidate the position, but the information had been distorted by a false assumption: that Iraq, like Egypt in 1973, would not attack.

———

In another part of Washington someone else was about to play an important role in the hardening of the American position: John Kelly. At eight o'clock that morning he was at his desk. He was annoyed. For twenty minutes he had been trying in vain to contact the Egyptian Ambassador in Washington. Nobody knew where he was. After half an hour he finally discovered that the Ambassador and his chargé d'affaires were in Cairo. He then sent a message directly to the Foreign Ministry in the Egyptian capital. It was such a forceful message that it is highly unlikely he could have acted without having been given the go-ahead by his superiors. "The West has done its duty, but the Arab nations are doing nothing. The United States has sold a lot of arms to Arab countries, especially Egypt. If they do not act, if they do not take a firm stand on the Kuwait affair, they can be sure that in future they will no longer be able to count on America."

The State Department denies that any message or phone call was sent to Cairo that day. But a highly placed and eminently trustworthy Egyptian source is adamant that he himself saw the message. The great mystery is whether the State Department was ever informed of the details of the conversation between President Bush and King Hussein when the U.S. President had agreed not to intervene with any Arab nations for forty-eight hours. If the State Department had not received this information, it was logically following the orders given by Bush to Brent Scowcroft at 5 A.M. on August 2, telling the State Department to put pressure on Arab states to condemn Saddam Hussein's invasion of Kuwait.

There was total amazement among Egyptian officials, but King Hussein knew nothing of this development when he landed in Amman. It was 2:00 P.M. in the Jordanian capital.

As he got out of the plane, the King was told he had an urgent call from his Foreign Minister, Marwan Al Qasim. When the King picked up the phone, he told Al Qasim: "I have very good news. Saddam Hussein has told me he's going to withdraw from Kuwait."

He was going to be more specific about his meeting with the Iraqi leader, but the Foreign Minister interrupted him. "You haven't heard, but the Egyptian Foreign Ministry has just put out a statement condemning the Iraqis for invading Kuwait."

King Hussein was shocked. "This destroys everything. And it gives all chances of broadening the conflict."

The King rushed to the palace and immediately tried to put in a call to President Mubarak. He had trouble getting him on the line. When he finally reached Mubarak, he told him of Saddam Hussein's agreement to pull out of Kuwait and to attend the mini-summit. "Why did you release that communiqué? We had agreed not to do something like that until the mini-summit took place."

Mubarak sounded confused. "I was under tremendous pressure from the media and my own people. My mind is not functioning."

The King shouted into the telephone: "Well, when it starts functioning again, call me."

In conversations with other people Mubarak would later give a totally different story about his conversation with King Hussein. "I asked King Hussein: Did he promise to withdraw unilaterally from Kuwait?"

According to the Egyptian President, the King replied; "No, but he will if a solution can be found during the mini-summit, especially if he obtains Kuwaiti concessions through the mediation of the Saudis."

"But did he clearly commit himself to withdrawal?"

"No."

Mubarak claims that this conversation convinced him that, as Saddam Hussein had given no guarantee that he would withdraw from Kuwait, even if agreement were reached at the mini-summit, there was no need for the latter to take place.

Highly placed figures within Iraq told us that, during the course of his meetings with King Hussein, the Iraqi President had agreed to go to Jeddah for a mini-summit on August 4 to negotiate with King Fahd and, if the negotiations were successful, to withdraw from Kuwait. Just before the war broke out, when Saddam Hussein was meeting with UN Secretary-General Pérez de Cuéllar in Baghdad, he re-emphasized his decision to pull out of Kuwait on August 5 if the mini-summit planned for August 4 in Jeddah were successful. We have further confirmed through top sources in Jordan that Saddam Hussein did indeed tell King Hussein that he was ready to pull out of Kuwait and that King Hussein passed this message to President Hosni Mubarak. This indicates that when Mubarak told Yasser Arafat that King Hussein had told him there had never been any agreement from Saddam Hussein to pull out of Kuwait, he was not telling the truth.

In Moscow Dennis Ross was losing patience. Since early morning James Baker's deputy, who was staying at the U.S. Ambassador's residence, had been fighting inch by inch for changes to be made in the text of the joint communiqué that was to be read by Baker and Shevardnadze. The draft that the Minister's colleague, Tarasenko, had brought him was unusable, too vague in its wording and too conciliatory in its tone. He told Tarasenko, "You'll have to have it rewritten. It must be stronger."

Tarasenko left and returned three hours later with a version that was equally unsatisfactory.

"You know what'll happen," said Ross after looking through

it. "If we use this text, we won't be sending the right message to Saddam Hussein. He won't see how united and how determined we are."

"I agree," replied Tarasenko, "but we're up against a certain amount of resistance. The Arab experts in our Ministry are opposed to the idea of abandoning an established partner like Iraq."

Tarasenko left again. After several more hours' wait, he returned triumphant. There was no time to lose: James Baker's plane was about to touch down. The two men bundled themselves into a limousine and set off for the airport at top speed. Ross read the text and at last found it satisfactory. He observed that one passage, calling for a joint embargo on arms sales, had been deleted. He pointed it out to Tarasenko. "Oh, that's nothing," the Soviet replied. "Your Secretary of State can discuss that with Comrade Shevardnadze."

They arrived just before Baker's Boeing landed. Shevardnadze was waiting on the tarmac. The two men shook hands, and Shevardnadze said, with an embarrassed smile: "I was wrong, Jim, when I told you there wouldn't be an invasion." Then, flanked by Ross and Tarasenko, they headed immediately for a heavily guarded room in the airport.

Baker was the first to speak: "It must be clear to Saddam Hussein and the rest of the world that we are together on this." Shevardnadze, who was usually prolix, agreed but without a great deal of warmth. After listening to what Baker had to say the Soviet minister replied: "We insist that the Soviet Union won't accept any gunboat diplomacy on your part."

Baker tried to reassure him: "There won't be any unilateral action by the United States unless American citizens are in danger."

Shevardnadze nodded, only half-convinced, and repeated: "Above all, no American military operations."

Jeddah, early evening. The number-two Iraqi, Izzat Ibrahim, arrived in Saudi Arabia for talks with King Fahd. Meanwhile, spy satellites revealed that elite troops of the Iraqi Republican Guard had just reached the border between Kuwait and Saudi Arabia.

In Amman King Hussein was shattered. He felt humiliated and deeply disheartened. In the King's eyes the Egyptian communiqué was all part of a vast conspiracy hatched by certain Arab countries to sabotage his efforts and prevent the mini-summit from being held the next day.

For several hours this man, so used to action and struggle, remained alone in his palace. The only visitor whom he agreed to see was his brother, Prince Hassan.

"The Arabs ought to have proved that they could settle the conflict themselves," he told the Prince, in a dejected tone. "We shouldn't have failed. Anything can happen now. We must expect the worst."

In the almost empty palace the telephone had stopped ringing. No leaders were calling Amman. During the hours spent alone, as he began to doubt everything, including himself, the King even considered abdicating.

He could hear noises rising from the city. Demonstrations in support of Saddam Hussein were taking place, and his own name was being hailed alongside that of the Iraqi leader. The demonstrators, most of them Palestinians, were proclaiming their hatred of the Gulf states. "Kuwait isn't a country; it isn't a people; it isn't a capital; it isn't even a town. It's just an oil well in the middle of the desert. These arrogant Gulf states refuse to grant citizenship to the Arabs who work for them and who have served them loyally for years. Saddam Hussein must invade Saudi Arabia too."

For the King these demonstrations of support were a "bitter victory." As night fell on the hills surrounding Amman, he had a premonition of the divisions that were about to tear the Arab world apart.

Meanwhile in Cairo the Arab League was ending the truce that King Hussein had demanded for the achievement of his efforts at mediation. The Foreign Ministers adopted a resolution condemning Iraq and calling for its troops to withdraw to the border unconditionally. Seven of the twenty-one members refused to vote for the resolution. They were—apart from Iraq—Jordan, Libya, Yemen, Sudan, Djibouti and the PLO. Just before the vote the Libyan Foreign Minister had slipped out of the room.

The delegates were not unaware that strong American pressure had been exerted on Mubarak all day—pressure on the order of John Kelly's message to Cairo. Egypt and Israel were the two countries in the region that benefited most from American financial aid—to the tune of $2 billion a year.

Although the resolution also called for an Arab summit to be organized "in order to discuss the aggression and to seek means to reach a permanent solution," any immediate hope of an Arab settlement had faded. According to the King of Jordan, Saddam Hussein had declared himself ready to discuss withdrawal from Kuwait at a mini-summit, on condition that the Arab League did not condemn him. The mini-summit that was due to be held the following day, August 4, was therefore, *de facto,* canceled. What much of the world was not told was that the resolution adopted by the Arab League that night also called for Western powers not to deploy any troops on Arab soil. Countries like Saudi Arabia, Egypt, and Syria voted for that resolution and that clause. The United States would turn around their position in the next week.

7

"I Wouldn't Invade
Saudi Arabia"

Reports arriving early on August 4 indicated that Iraqi troops
had entered the "neutral zone" between Kuwait and Saudi
Arabia and were taking up position about half a mile from the
Saudi border. At National Security Agency headquarters at
Fort Meade photos taken by spy satellites, which were now
photographing every mile of the crisis zone, showed that
100,000 soldiers of Iraq's élite troops were now massed near
the border. They belonged both to the Third Army Corps and
to the Republican Guard, which also provided personal protection for Saddam Hussein and possessed eight divisions of
between thirty and thirty-three brigades each.

A secret report was passed to the main members of the administration, evaluating the dangers posed by these forces:

An Iraqi invasion of Saudi Arabia would involve a much
more extensive military operation than those so far conducted by Baghdad's ground forces. The key objectives of

the invasion would be the ports and airfields near Dharan (one of the main petroleum centers), about 175 miles from the Kuwaiti border, with the capital, Riyadh, as the next objective. This area contains all the vital economic targets whose capture would cut off Saudi access to the Persian Gulf and hamper the arrival of American reinforcements.

The study considered the various offensives that might be conducted on Saudi territory by the Republican Guard and ended with an unexpected historical comparison:

The excellent reputation of the Republican Guard could be a serious weak point. Their destruction, or a serious defeat, would be a major shock to the morale of the rest of the army and could precipitate its disintegration. It is not inconceivable that the Iraqi forces might react in the same way as the French army at the Battle of Waterloo when it learned of the retreat of Napoleon's old guard. The cry of "the guard is retreating" provoked panic in the French army and led to its immediate collapse.

At Camp David, the President's summer retreat in the Catoctin Mountains, the second meeting called by George Bush in less than twenty-four hours began at eight in the morning. Besides Brent Scowcroft, Richard Haas, and General Colin Powell, who had been present the day before, there were White House Chief of Staff John Sununu, Treasury Secretary Nicholas Brady, CIA Director William Webster, and Secretary of State James Baker, who had returned from Moscow the previous evening. Sitting around an oak table in a log cabin, most of those present had exchanged their business suits and dark ties for more casual clothes, as if they had come for a long, relaxing weekend. In reality, they were in the middle of a rapidly escalating crisis.

A number of military experts who had been summoned to the meeting began with a briefing whose subject was "The situation as it is on the ground and what we can do about it."

The possibility of clandestine action, designed to destabilize the Iraqi regime or to remove Saddam Hussein, was brought up, but no specific plans were discussed. When the military men had finished they left the room, and George Bush asked his colleagues for their comments. Everything revolved around the military options. It was clear that an American military deployment in the Gulf could not be put into operation without the support of the Arab countries, in particular Saudi Arabia. But Riyadh was not yet ready to give the go-ahead, for two reasons: the Saudis were still clinging to the possibility of an Arab settlement, and the idea of American troops on their soil made them deeply uneasy.

The latest news about Iraqi troops massing on the Saudi border was both a further worry and also, above all, a trump card in negotiations with King Fahd. George Bush was quite clear on that point. He had often shown his irritation since the beginning of the crisis: he was disappointed at the slowness of the international response and angered by the violent repression being carried out by the Iraqis in Kuwait.

When Colin Powell began to speak the President settled into his armchair with a set expression on his face, his hands joined, the tips of his fingers touching his nose. He was going to hear the military option.

Since August 2nd, General Norman Schwarzkopf, nicknamed "the Bear" because of his imposing physique, had been sleeping no more than a few hours a night. He had been smoking more than usual and had hardly set foot outside his headquarters at MacDill, a U.S. Air Force base in Florida. An ex-football player, who had been known at West Point as someone who liked to live well, Schwarzkopf was the head of CENTCOM. The Pentagon strategists divided the world into zones of responsibility. The zone covered by CENTCOM was an area of 15 million square miles stretching from Kenya to Pakistan. Seventy percent of all the world's oil reserves were situated in the region for which the gruffly jovial general was responsible.

Since the beginning of the crisis he had been working in constant liaison with the Chiefs of Staff and Colin Powell. He had been given a clear objective: to adapt the famous secret plan 90-1002, conceived by the Carter Administration for military intervention in the Gulf, for a massive defense of Saudi Arabia.

"The Bear" and his associates were faced with a multitude of problems. The most serious were the lack of bases on Saudi territory and the consistently high temperatures in the desert, which made fighting particularly difficult. Other causes of anxiety were the possibility that the Iraqis might use chemical weapons and that the first, relatively unprotected, troops might be decimated before the tanks and heavy material had arrived.

An intervention in the Gulf was probably the most difficult challenge the American military authorities had had to face since the Vietnam war. In the last week of July a exercise called "War Flag 90" had been organized in order to test the ability of the Army chiefs to communicate at long distances. The operation had been oriented toward the Middle East, but despite the growing tension in the region Iraq, Kuwait, and Saudi Arabia had not been named. In order not to offend anyone's sensibilities, General Colin Powell, with exceptional tact, had even asked for the maps to be cut and altered. The result was that they bore absolutely no resemblance to the countries of the region.

At MacDill base and at the Pentagon giant computers were working around the clock, constantly assessing new data. A huge program was now being developed with the enigmatic name of TPFD: Time Phase Force Deployment. It would contain details of the forces and equipment to be sent, the means to transport them, all the communications systems to coordinate the operation, and everything needed by the troops in the Saudi desert: aerial defense, drinking water, quarters, etc.

Schwarzkopf and Powell were both Vietnam veterans, both cautious about the use of force and both convinced that a military operation could succeed only if it were conducted on a large scale, with vast means, and supported by an unfaltering determination on the part of the politicians.

The office of the Chairman of the Joint Chiefs of Staff contained a chart, displayed in a prominent position, listing "The Rules of Colin Powell," thirteen maxims, one of which was "Choose carefully what you want. You can get it."

At Camp David that morning, when he began to address George Bush and the members of the Administration, Powell had to hand all the data provided for him by Schwarzkopf.

"Mr. President," he said, "if you decide on military action, commit our forces *en masse* and in a fit manner. It's clear that Saddam Hussein doesn't want a confrontation with the United States. He's a brute but not a fool. He knows that he'd lose a large-scale war with America. If military intervention takes place, sizable forces must be sent immediately to Saudi Arabia to demonstrate our determination to defend the kingdom. The deployment must also be large enough to let Saddam Hussein know that to attack Saudi Arabia would be to attack the Americans. Plan 90-1002 must give us control of the air and the ability to commit troops in sufficient numbers to deter but also to fight. No nation has ever gained advantage from a prolonged conflict."

This was the kind of thing the President wanted to hear. After quickly getting comments from the others around the table, Bush made his decision. He gave the go-ahead for Plan 90-1002 to be implemented and for the greatest armada since the Vietnam war to be sent to the other side of the world. The President, according to an eyewitness, "had become a real hawk," only leaving Colin Powell to take care of the details. The first troops would not leave until the beginning of the following week, and until then the operation would remain top secret.

There was one major obstacle still to be overcome: Saudi Arabia had to agree. Bush asked Defense Secretary Cheney to get ready to leave for Jeddah the following day. Brent Scowcroft suggested that he be accompanied by Robert Gates, number two at the National Security Council, who had previously been Deputy Director of the CIA. General Schwarzkopf would also be in the delegation.

The meeting ended at 10:15 A.M. It was decided that a final meeting would be held at the White House the following afternoon.

Meanwhile Yasser Arafat was meeting Mubarak. The Egyptian President was tense and kept saying angrily, "Iraq must withdraw." He talked of his conversation the previous day with King Hussein, who had just come from Baghdad. Mubarak spoke as if he were trying to justify his position, come what may. "I asked him if he'd discussed with Saddam Hussein his withdrawal from Kuwait. He said, no, all they'd discussed was the holding of a mini-summit in Jeddah, to be attended by King Fahd, King Hussein, myself, and Saddam Hussein, who'd agreed to the idea. I replied that I wouldn't go as long as Saddam Hussein hadn't promised to withdraw."

Mubarak's words contradicted those of King Hussein, who

had stated that the Iraqi President had told him he would withdraw if an agreement could be reached at the mini-summit.

Throughout the discussion Mubarak seemed embarrassed, probably because no one in the Arab world was unaware that he had been under enormous pressure from the Americans. At one point in the conversation he confided to Arafat that a military operation would be launched against Iraq between the twelfth and eighteenth of August. The PLO chief was surprised but did not ask him where he had got his information from.

At the end of their talk, Arafat said, "You ought to go Saudi Arabia and Iraq."

Mubarak's blunt response was "You go first." Then, after a few moments' reflection, he added, "Yes, you go and see if Saddam is ready to withdraw. Then I'll go."

At 8:00 P.M. King Fahd was talking to some of his close aides in the gardens of his residence in Jeddah when one of his colleagues came across the lawn towards him. "Your Majesty, the President of the United States is on the phone."

Bush was calling from Camp David, where it was 1:00 P.M. The first words he spoke to Fahd were those used by Margaret Thatcher in Aspen two days earlier: "Your Majesty, you know, he's not going to stop."

He passed on to the King the latest information he had received about Iraqi troop concentrations on the Saudi border. Fahd seemed anxious and disoriented, and this time he was much more receptive to Bush's proposals. As a member of the White House staff put it: "Up until then, the Arabs had been paralyzed with fear." Now this fear had become a trump card in Bush's strategy concerning the Saudis.

The conversation between the two leaders lasted quite a while. The Saudi army, with only 65,000 men, could not hope to stand up to the force of Iraqi firepower; the troops massed on the border were, according to Bush, élite units in an offensive posture. (This was later to prove inaccurate.) It was essential for the kingdom to think of defending itself, and Washington could provide sizable military support. The President suggested sending the U.S. Defense Secretary to see King Fahd with "a bundle of reports from the intelligence services proving that an Iraqi invasion was a real danger, and also with specific plans for the deployment of American troops on your territory."

Fahd agreed to receive Cheney but asked Bush for another twenty-four hours in which to think before agreeing to an American military presence.

George Bush emerged from this conversation with increased confidence. He spent much of the rest of the day telephoning his principal colleagues as well as a number of foreign heads of state, notably President Ozal of Turkey.

Turkey was a NATO ally but also a country through which 1.6 million barrels of oil a day passed: half of all Iraq's petroleum exports. There were 750 miles of pipeline leading from the Kirkuk oil fields to the terminals at Yumurtalik on the Mediterranean coast. The current crisis had put Turkey's leaders in a difficult position. Transporting Iraqi oil earned Turkey $300 million a year, and Iraq also supplied Turkey with two-thirds of her energy needs. The nation's press had unanimously condemned the invasion, but in private officials were more hesitant. Any step toward either side could cost Turkey dearly. Bush pointed out to Ozal that international action against Iraq depended largely on cutting off her oil exports. He added that he had already made the same request of the Saudis, who had agreed.

It was a premature assertion. Bush preferred to wait for all the military questions to be settled before tackling that problem with Riyadh. Saudi Arabia was the country through which the other half of Iraq's oil exports passed.

Ozal, a plump man with a round face and glasses, was a skillful tactician. He considered it prudent to wait and see how the situation developed. He assured Bush of his support but gave him no firm commitment and neglected to tell him that the following day he would be receiving an envoy from Saddam Hussein. After his conversation with Bush, Ozal called Iraq's mortal enemy, Iranian President Rafsanjani. That same day information from official sources in Tehran would reveal that, two weeks before, Saddam Hussein had contacted Rafsanjani with a view to negotiating Iran's neutrality if Kuwait were to be invaded.

In Amman, King Hussein uttered a word that was to isolate him still further from most of the Arab governments and from his American ally. After criticizing the attitudes of the countries in the region and their condemnation of Iraq, he added: "Saddam Hussein is a patriot."

On Sunday, August 5, Yasser Arafat met Saddam Hussein in Baghdad. The Iraqi leader claimed to be "shocked" that the mini-summit had been canceled. He even asked Arafat, "In your opinion, who sabotaged it?"

Saddam's attitudes and statements that day revealed a strange mixture of bitterness and determination. He spent a long time justifying his invasion of Kuwait and spoke of his disappointment at Arab reaction. But Arafat noted that his morale did not seem in the least shaken. Saddam was calm, occasionally quite lively, and he even made a few jokes. "A political solution is absolutely essential," he told Arafat.

"I completely agree."

Saddam was silent for a few moments and then added, "Go and see the Saudis, and tell them we're ready to talk."

The same day a prominent Palestinian businessman got an urgent call from Baghdad. Nizar Hamdoon, the Deputy Foreign Minister, was on the line. "You've got to come to Baghdad as soon as possible. It is urgent." The businessman was not enthusiastic about making the trip to the Iraqi capital but said he would talk to Hamdoon again. The next day Hamdoon called again. During the conversation the businessman learned that Arafat was going to Vienna on August 7 to attend the funeral of the former Austrian Chancellor, Bruno Kreisky. He said he would go to Vienna to meet Arafat and that whatever message Hamdoon wanted to get to him should be given to Arafat to pass on.

On the 7th they met in Vienna, and Arafat handed the businessman, who had highly placed contacts inside the White House in Washington, a message from Saddam Hussein to President George Bush. The message confirmed that Saddam Hussein was ready to pull out of Kuwait but needed to resolve problems with Kuwait first.

The businessman called John Sununu, the White House Chief of Staff and told him he was forwarding the message. "It's OK, but I don't want anyone to know such a message has been passed on," Sununu said. When the message got to Washington, there was no reply.

That Sunday a secret meeting of Israel's ministerial defense committee was held in Jerusalem.

Prime Minister Shamir was in a bad mood. The "special relationship" between his country and Washington had reached an all-time low. "Bush has phoned all his allies," Shamir had told his colleagues, "and practically every leader in the region, except those of Libya, Iraq, Iran, the PLO . . . and Israel."

The attitude of the Bush administration was a worrying thing
for the Israeli leaders. It was clear to them that the Americans
wanted to keep Israel on the sidelines and force her to maintain
a low profile in order not to threaten the anti-Iraq Arab coalition
that was being formed. All Jerusalem's offers to cooperate with
Washington, especially with regard to intelligence, had so far
gone unacknowledged.

The atmosphere of the secret meeting was grim. Defense
Minister Moshe Arens stated, "We must reserve the right to
intervene if the geo-strategic situation in the Middle East
changes drastically or if Jordan is invaded."

Among those present were the Chief of Staff, General Dan
Shomron, who had led the successful raid on Entebbe, and the
heads of the intelligence services. Nobody believed that Saudi
Arabia would be invaded. "The scale of international reaction,"
said one of the participants, "makes such an attack unlikely." On
the other hand, it was considered highly likely, and worrying,
that Iraqi forces might mass on the Jordanian border. Iraqi
missiles were even now on their way to the Jordanian border
—missiles that could reach Jerusalem or Tel Aviv in four minutes.

"We have to increase our intelligence-gathering activities in
Iraq," said Shamir. "We have to get information from there at
a high level, so that we know what's happening when it happens
and not the day after."

The jibe was directed at the heads of the intelligence services.
Since August 2 the failings of Israeli intelligence with regard to
the crisis had been much discussed, especially in the press. Now
Saddam Hussein's tactics were carefully dissected by those present
at the meeting, and a curious parallel emerged.

In 1980, on the eve of the Iraqi offensive against the Fao
peninsula that would mark the beginning of the Iran–Iraq war,
Saddam had gone to inspect his troops on a distant front in
order to give the impression that the attack would take place

in a different area. Ten years later he had invited all the foreign military attachés in Baghdad to observe the two divisions he had stationed on the border with Kuwait. It had been a brilliant red herring. Who could possibly believe that a country that had invited foreign experts to observe its military disposition was about to launch an invasion? Immediately after the military attachés had returned to Baghdad Saddam Hussein had given the order for the main body of his army to move against the Emirate, while Western and Arab embassies were sending reassuring and optimistic cables to their capitals.

One thing was now obvious: Israel sorely lacked a military satellite able to detect enemy troop movements from a long distance away. The Americans would have to be asked for immediate help in realizing such a project.

After the meeting Foreign Minister David Levy closeted himself with Shamir and Moshe Arens. Levy was leaving for Washington the next day, and now was the time to finalize the details of the Israeli position on all the subjects that would be discussed. The trip was coming at exactly the right moment. It would give them the opportunity to sound out American intentions regarding the Gulf crisis. A few hours later Shamir and Levy were dismayed to hear from James Baker that he was postponing the Foreign Minister's visit for a month.

Late that afternoon the helicopter bringing George Bush back from Camp David touched down on the White House lawn. The President got out, reading a note that had just been handed to him by Richard Haas, who was at his side. The scribbled note read: "President Ozal of Turkey is on the phone." Some journalists who were waiting nearby called to him. Bush hesitated for a moment, then walked toward them. He seemed nervous. "The occupation of Kuwait won't last," he said.

Although an important ally was waiting to speak to him, Bush spent the next twenty minutes answering the journalists' questions. One of the questions made him lose his temper briefly. To his statement, "We have the support of the Arab world," a journalist responded, "How can you say that when every newspaper is carrying a picture of Saddam Hussein with the King of Jordan on its front page?"

Bush's brusque reply was "I can read. What's your question?"

He retreated to the Oval Office, where messages of support from all over the United States were waiting for him. Some of the messages were terse in the extreme: "Go to it" or "Kick him out." As one of Bush's aides put it, "America is getting impatient."

Defense Secretary Cheney had just left Washington for Saudi Arabia and Egypt. The meeting with King Fahd was considered crucial. "The case we're putting to the Saudis," a member of the White House staff would say, "is perfectly clear-cut. We're telling him, listen, here's a guy who lied to you about what he was going to do five days before he did it. There's no reason to believe him this time. You know the saying: 'Once bitten, twice shy.' "

Another off-the-record statement by a highly placed official sheds light on American objectives: "The occupation of Kuwait isn't, in itself, a threat to American interests. The real threat lies in the power Iraq would have in possessing 20 percent of the world's resources of oil, controlling OPEC, dominating the Middle East, threatening Israel and wanting to acquire the atomic bomb."

By early evening Bush had scored an impressive record. In four days he had made twenty-three phone calls to twelve foreign leaders, sometimes at the rate of one call every two hours. Now, before returning to his apartments, he phoned Colin Powell and gave him the authorization to begin assembling all the troops who could possibly be sent to Saudi Arabia. Soon afterward he had a final meeting with James Baker and Brent Scowcroft to discuss the last remaining stumbling block: the reaction of the Soviet Union.

Bush had planned to give the final go-ahead for the sending of troops on Monday evening, after Richard Cheney's meeting with King Fahd. The first forces would leave on Tuesday morning, but the President hoped to wait until Wednesday to make a public announcement.

The three men agreed that it would be a disaster if Moscow were faced with a *fait accompli*. If Gorbachev criticized the deployment publicly, all the efforts being made to persuade the United Nations to agree to sanctions would be in jeopardy. The UN vote was due to take place the following afternoon. Scowcroft suggested that they take advantage of this "short but sufficient" time to inform and reassure Moscow about American intentions. "We can use the urgency of the situation," said Scowcroft, "to cement Soviet–American relations more quickly." It was decided that Baker would exploit the time difference and call Shevardnadze in Moscow late that evening.

Powell, Baker, Scowcroft: by virtue of being constantly in the front line in the management of the crisis, the three men formed a virtual war cabinet. They were very different in character.

Colin Powell was, to quote one of his friends, "a real dream for the PR men" and a living embodiment of the American Dream. The son of Jamaican immigrants, he had grown up in Harlem and the South Bronx. His school record had been unimpressive. At elementary school he had been placed in a class for "slow" pupils. Everything changed in the army. He distinguished himself in Vietnam and was awarded eleven medals. His hard line on the "Soviet threat" brought him to the attention of Reagan's entourage. Powell entered the White House and had no difficulty in negotiating the transition from Reagan to

Bush. On being appointed a four-star general and the Chairman of the Joint Chiefs of Staff, he stated, a touch provocatively: "I've risen through the army hierarchy without playing bridge, golf, or tennis."

James Baker—the third of that name, as he liked to point out—was, like his best friend George Bush, heir to a fortune. Bush had studied at Yale, Baker at Princeton. His family's money, which came from a prominent law practice in Houston, allowed him to embark on a successful career in business and politics. As White House Chief of Staff under Ronald Reagan, then as Treasury Secretary, he was a constant companion of the future President at dinners and weekends and on fishing expeditions. Although his tone was as restrained as that of Bush, his replies were often more incisive, and he occasionally let his emotions show in an unexpected way.

Brent Scowcroft was halfway between the other two in character. A taciturn man of sixty-five, the ex-Air Force general was known as an "intellectual soldier" with a sharp mind. Deeply loyal to Bush, he had seen at close hand the rivalry that had existed under various presidents between the head of the National Security Council—his own present post—and the Secretary of State. He knew that the latter had usually emerged the winner, which was probably why he had chosen to keep a lower profile than Baker, who was hungrier for media attention. But Scowcroft was a key man, a real *eminence grise* whose astuteness he may have inherited from his former boss and mentor, Henry Kissinger. Since the beginning of the crisis he had hardly ever left the President's side, preparing his statements and speeches, analyzing intelligence reports in detail and weighing carefully the pros and cons of each decision.

August 6. Eduard Shevardnadze was spending a few days' vacation at his *dacha* in the Crimea. He was at home alone, relaxing, when the telephone rang. One of his colleagues was calling from Moscow. "The American Secretary of State wants to speak to you."

Ten minutes later Baker was on the line. He sounded cheerful. "How's your vacation, Shev? Is the weather fine?" After some more small talk, the American's tone changed. "We're going to have to send troops to the Gulf." He added immediately: "At the request of Saudi Arabia."

He spoke of the latest reports from the intelligence services on the continuing Iraqi military buildup, both in Kuwait and on the Saudi border, where more than 100,000 men were now massed. Shevardnadze listened in silence. "We give you our assurance," Baker continued, "that we're not trying to take advantage of the situation in order to increase our influence in the region."

"What's the point of this call, Jim? To consult us or to inform us?" Shevardnadze's voice was ice cold.

"We're informing you," replied Baker, embarrassed, "because I don't think it's something we could do together. Or would you like to think about that? I don't have the authority to suggest it, but would you consider cooperating by sending naval or land forces?"

Baker had already mentioned the idea the previous day to the Saudis, and they had not been opposed to a Soviet presence. Shevardnadze said nothing, and Baker put the question another way: "Shev, what could we do to cooperate on this problem?"

"Why not work within the military committee of the United Nations?"

The Soviets had been trying for years to reactivate this UN body, which had long been dormant.

Immediately after this conversation Baker spoke to Bush with great enthusiasm about the idea of Soviet military involvement in the Gulf crisis. Bush said that he was interested and immediately called Colin Powell, who had no objection to such an initiative.

Excited, Baker called Shevardnadze back. "President Bush can see no obstacle to a naval or land presence of the Soviet Union in that region."

"All right," said Shevardnadze, who seemed more guarded in his response. "If President Bush is really interested, I'll discuss it with President Gorbachev."

From a diplomatic point of view, the idea was revolutionary, but as things turned out, nobody was to be very happy about it.

"It's a major advance," Baker told his entourage. "First there was the joint communiqué that we read in Moscow, in which the Soviets broke with one of their oldest allies and condemned him. Now we're suggesting to them that they become politically and militarily involved in the Gulf."

But as soon as news of the proposal leaked out of the narrow circle of Baker's close colleagues, what amounted to a revolt swept the State Department. For decades the aim of American diplomacy had been to keep the Soviets out of the Middle East. Baker's initiative broke with this dogma. Memos, either worried or angry, began to arrive on his desk from various sections of the State Department. The Department's bureaucrats were to find an unexpected ally. Gorbachev was far from grateful for the proposal. The scale of the internal difficulties he had to face and the bitter memory of the incursion into Afghanistan encouraged the Kremlin leadership to adopt a cautious wait-and-see policy.

"This offer is a token of our good faith," Baker told Shevardnadze a few days later.

"Thank you," the Soviet replied, tersely. "We've been aware of that."

Late that morning Arafat returned to Cairo, where he was joined by the PLO's number two, Abu Iyad, in further talks with President Mubarak. Arafat told Mubarak of his interview with Saddam Hussein the previous day: "He really is ready to negotiate." He added that he was ever more fearful of a military confrontation. According to Abu Iyad, it was quite possible that the Israelis would intervene. Mubarak seemed to have become more and more hostile to Iraq and opposed to all compromise. To the PLO chief Mubarak's new hard line was the product of the violent political and media offensive launched by the United States. The two Palestinians planned to fly next to Saudi Arabia, the one country still able to work for a negotiated settlement.

In Jeddah, Richard Cheney was putting the finishing touches to the agreement he had reached with King Fahd. In fact, Cheney had become more of a negotiator than a messenger in the current crisis. He had only been Bush's second choice for the key post of Defense Secretary; his nomination had been proposed and supported by Brent Scowcroft. Cheney suffered from a heart condition, and when Scowcroft had met him to discuss the possibility of his nomination, the first blunt question he had asked was: "Dick, how's your health?"

The ground had, to a large extent, been prepared by President Bush's telephone conversations with the King. General Schwarzkopf and Robert Gates were present at the talks, as were Fahd's brother and Defense Minister, Prince Sultan, who had cut short his convalescence in Morocco, and Abdullah Bin Abdullaziz, heir to the throne, Deputy Prime Minister and commander of the Bedouin Guard. Abdullah had always been more skeptical about the United States than Fahd. He was the man to convince. He studied carefully the reports from the American secret services and the satellite photos showing details of Iraqi troop concentrations in Kuwait and on the Saudi border, and he spoke at length with Schwarzkopf and Cheney about possible sites where American troops might be stationed.

"This is the whole of what we can offer you and provide you with," said Cheney.

"All right," Fahd said finally. "I'll take all of it."

The Saudi leaders had stipulated one precondition before they would give their final agreement: "It is out of the question for military bases to be established permanently on our soil."

The American delegation had foreseen this objection and proposed a secret protocol: U.S. troops would withdraw from Saudi territory as soon as events allowed, but permanent bases housing both U.S. troops and those of the multinational force would be established in the Emirate of Bahrain, not far from the coast of Saudi Arabia, as well as inside liberated Kuwait.

The Americans were counting on the Saudi leaders' discontent. There was, first of all, the problem of King Fahd, who seemed less and less capable of taking action. As a disillusioned colleague put it, "As soon as a problem arises, the King runs away from it." Fahd was spending more time alone in his palace, avoiding his advisers and his family alike. The Saudi leaders had also taken the measure of their own vulnerability: in the past few years they had bought more than $150 billion worth of sophisticated armaments, yet they had to admit that they would be incapable of resisting an offensive by a powerfully armed country like Iraq. Jeddah had been using its formidable oil revenues—nearly $50 billion a year—in trying to forge regional alliances and to neutralize possible enemies. The Gulf crisis had revealed the shortcomings of this strategy.

While the talks between the Americans and the Saudis were beginning in Jeddah, Saddam Hussein was receiving the American chargé d'affaires in Baghdad, Joseph Wilson. The diplomat was greeted by a relaxed Saddam, whose first question was "What is the political and diplomatic news?"

Wilson turned toward the Information Minister, who was present at the interview. "Your Minister, through CNN [Cable News Network], has more information than I."

Saddam Hussein said: "I asked you to study the latest developments after our meeting with your Ambassador. After that meeting the negotiations between us and the previous government in Kuwait failed, and whatever happened happened."

"Your Minister informed me at an earlier stage," Wilson replied.

The President continued:

I am informed on the American position in detail. We know that whenever something happens in the Arab world, Europe, Asia or Latin America the U.S. takes a position, and we are not surprised when the U.S. condemns such action, especially when the U.S. is not part of it. But I have to say that the U.S. has to be careful not to listen to bad advice. It could place the U.S. in a difficult position.

I am sure that you have read and seen our letters to Iran during the war, and those letters include an appraisal of the situation both present and future. Because those letters were very frank, the Iranians thought they were tactical. But we told them what we thought because we wanted peace, and war was causing us sorrow. And you know the results: if the advice we had given the Iranians had been taken into account, the war would not have happened.

I will talk about the relationship between Iraq and the U.S. in view of the developments, and what will happen in the future if the U.S. makes any mistakes. To start with, I would like to talk about three points that are linked to the present situation.

Kuwait was a state without any real frontier. Even before 1961 it was not a state. What happened in 1961? When Abdul Karim Kassem appointed a governor to Kuwait, under the authority of the province of Basra, both the Iranians and Abdul Karim knew that Kuwait was part of Iraq. So, up to now, Kuwait was a state without borders, and whatever happened with the entry of the Iraqi forces cannot be measured in the framework of the relationship between states in the Arab world.

You know that we have with Saudi Arabia an excellent relationship that started in 1975, and it was developing well before August 2. Trust and co-ordination between us was evolving at all levels before August 2, and, whatever the U.S. policy, we did not see that our good relations with Saudi Arabia were causing harm to U.S. interests. If that is correct, not only did the good relations between Iraq and Saudi Arabia not cause harm to the U.S., but they were one of the factors of stability in the area. So meddling in the relations between Iraq and Saudi Arabia will destabilize the area and damage U.S. interests.

We don't understand the meaning of your declarations that you are afraid of Iraq's intentions with respect to Saudi Arabia and that after Kuwait will come Saudi Arabia. There is one other point that we do not understand. If you want to preempt events and prompt Saudi Arabia to take action against Iraq, which will force Iraq to answer, perhaps your aim is to provoke.

You know that we were the first to propose a security

agreement with Saudi Arabia that precludes intervention in each other's internal affairs and recourse to force, and we signed that agreement. We proposed the same agreement to Kuwait, but they refused to sign the agreement with us, probably on the advice of a foreign power, possibly Britain.

You know also that some Western circles were annoyed and joked about the idea of those agreements, comparing them with agreements between Great Britain and France, for example [the Sykes–Picot agreement for the division of the Middle East after the First World War]. Thank God, Kuwait did not sign that agreement with us.

I was very happy when we decided to support the revolutionary group in Kuwait because there was no agreement between us and Kuwait. If there had been, we couldn't have done that.

Saudi Arabia helped us and supported us during the war with Iran. After an initiative from them we got the pipeline, and they even gave us financial support and not loans.

If you are really worried about Saudi Arabia, your worries are unfounded, but if you are showing that worry in order to worry Saudi Arabia, that is something else. We will say the same thing to our Saudi brothers, and we are ready to give them any guarantees that they want, to remove that worry. More than that, if there is a foreign danger, we feel that it is our duty to protect Saudi Arabia. As for our relationship with the Arab world, we can be reconciled with them one evening and disagree the next evening. Up to now we have not had any problems.

The third point I want to talk to you about is that there have been rumours that Saddam Hussein gave certain Arab officials a promise that he would not use force against Kuwait in any circumstances. We have learned also, in one

way and another, that certain Arab officials passed on to
the Americans such an understanding. I would like to stress
here that the Americans should not use those promises
against us. I did not give that promise to any Arab. What
happened is that some Arab leaders were talking to me
about the massing of troops on the Kuwaiti border, and
they were telling me that the Kuwaitis were afraid and
worried. I told them that I promised that I would not take
any military action before the meeting in Jeddah that we
had agreed upon. This is what happened. There was no
military action before the meeting. We were waiting for
the return of the Vice President from Jeddah to take a
decision.

There is some talk about the speed with which the operation was undertaken, implying that the intention was
there before the Jeddah meeting. That possibility arose
before the Jeddah meeting and in accordance with the pa-
triotic movement in Kuwait. But it was not the first priority
on the list. We were putting more effort into asserting our
rights through negotiation. We are Arabs, and it was natural that we would seek to have relations with the Kuwaiti
opposition, just as the Kuwaitis would contact the Iraqi
opposition if we attacked them.

When our essential interests were in danger, and when
all other avenues had been exhausted, we had to use military power. The question for the American President and
officials is now: where are American interests endangered,
in Kuwait or outside?

You know that you have been buying Iraqi oil since I
came to power, although our relationship has been severed
during that time, and you bought more oil after resuming
the relationship in 1984. Until you decided to boycott Iraqi
oil, you were buying about one-third of our oil output. This

is not a technical decision; it is a political one. We know that your interest lies in your trade and the continuing supply of oil. So what are you frightened of? What makes you discuss military options, which will surely fail?

You are a great power, and we know that you can harm us, as I have told your Ambassador before, but if that happens, you will lose the whole area, and you will not be able to bring us to our knees even if you use all your weapons. You can destroy our technical research, our economy, our oil, but the more you destroy, the more difficult it will become for you. After that we will not hesitate to attack your interests in the area, as we attacked Kuwait when it plotted against us. Don't put us in such a position again. When we see that our life is threatened, we will threaten others. We know that you are a great power, capable of doing harm and destroying, but nobody can destroy man but God.

Why do you want to be our enemies? You have made enough mistakes by weakening your allies in such a way that, in the eyes of their people, they have no influence in the area. In our view, you could look after your interests better through a strong nationalistic and realistic regime in the area than through the Saudis. You are talking about an aggressive Iraq, but if Iraq was aggressive during the Iran war, why did you maintain relations with it? You are talking about the April 2 communiqué: we never issued such a communiqué before, during or after the war with Iran.

Why did I issue that communiqué? It was because some Western and American circles were urging Israel to attack us, and its aim was to put an end to all aggression. We believe that it promoted peace. If we had remained silent, Israel would have attacked us, and we would have counterattacked. You will remember that during the war we were constantly bombarded by Iran, and when we got rockets we didn't use them at first but merely threatened to use them. If Iran had listened to our advice, we would not have used them. But, thank God, up to now Israel has listened to us. Has that saved the cause of peace? Baghdad can resist rockets better than Israel.

To conclude, if the U.S. President wants to maintain his policy in the area and preserve his interests, as we have discussed, then the military option and rising tension goes against those interests—unless there is something else behind the raising of tension. In any case, we want stability and peace, though we will not be suppressed. We hate famine and hunger. Our people were hungry for a thousand years, and we will not go back to that. We look forward with honour to a humanitarian future that includes building and developing good relations with the U.S.—if the U.S. wants. This is my new message to President Bush.

Wilson was finally able to reply. "Thank you, Mr. President. I will convey your words to my government, and I will transmit your message by telephone immediately; I will also put it on paper. As you have said, correctly, this is a dangerous time, not only for American–Iraqi relations but for stability in the area and in the world."

"Why dangerous for the world?" asked the President.

Wilson replied, "As I understand, there is a sense of insecurity and unrest in the world markets."

"That is your fault," retorted Saddam Hussein. "We accepted $25 a barrel, and if it were not for your boycott, the price of a barrel would be around $21. When you boycott 5 million barrels in one go, then instability occurs. We believe that all dealers will benefit from it but not the American people."

"I sense that I have touched a nerve here," Wilson replied.

"In fact, I wanted to say that during these difficult days it appears to me that it is important that we maintain dialogue between us to avoid making mistakes. That is the only way in which we are going to be able to remove tension and cool emotions. That is why I welcome this occasion to transmit this letter, but I would like to make two remarks and then return to the points that you have made. I will relay to you or to your Ministers President Bush's answer. First, in the first part of your message you mentioned that Kuwait is part of Iraq."

"This is our history," the President said. "When we say that, we say it to assure everyone that Kuwait should have taken that fact into account and not tried to circumvent it. This is the essence of the relationship between Iraq and Kuwait, and it is different for other countries like Egypt or Saudi Arabia."

"It is important for me to understand the nature of the relationship."

Saddam Hussein explained: "The relationship is defined by the relationship of the people of the countries and not by me, the Americans, Soviets or others. These relations must be built on brotherhood and mutual respect."

Wilson asked: "Were these missing from Iraq's relationship with Kuwait?"

"Yes," Saddam Hussein replied, "and especially in the last month. I chased Jaber in an attempt to define the borders, and he said, 'Let others do it.' We have documents to prove that. We found it strange then, but we found out afterwards that he was plotting against us."

"Thanks. My second point: you have talked about your fraternal relations with Saudi Arabia, and you mentioned your non-aggression pact with Saudi Arabia. I would like to inform you about the worry of our government *vis-à-vis* Iraq's intentions now. I feel that you have given a general answer to that concern, but permit me . . ."

:"What would dissipate your worries?" asked the President.

"I don't know, and I will ask my President. I know that you are a frank and upright person, but please let us agree that, in the conditions prevailing today, which have seen no military action on the part of the U.S. or the Saudis, I have your assurance that you do not intend to undertake any military action against Saudi Arabia."

Saddam Hussein replied: "You can offer that assurance to the Saudis and to the world. We will not attack those who do not attack us. We will not harm those who do not harm us. Those who want our friendship will find us more than eager to be friendly. As for Saudi Arabia, the question has not even crossed my mind. Our relationship is strong—tell me if you know something we don't. It is natural, and we are not annoyed, that King Fahd receives the former ruler of Kuwait, Sheikh Jaber. We will be annoyed only if they allow them to work against Iraq from Saudi Arabia. By the way, say hello to President Bush and tell him to consider the Jaber family, and the group that is with them, finished, history. The family of Sabah is history."

"It is legitimate," he continued, "for everyone to worry about his own interests, and we want to know exactly what the legitimate interests of the Americans are, so we can reassure them of the safety of those interests. I tell you that not for tactical reasons, not because you are boycotting us—I made a point only of seeing you after you boycotted us, and I am not seeking here to lift the boycott. I am not even trying to say that what we did has to be approved by the U.S., but I want to understand what the legitimate interests of the U.S. are and to advise it not to take any bold steps from which it could retreat."

"I will pass that on to my government," Wilson said. "I came here with three matters in mind that are the worries of my government. First, the nature of the invasion, and you know well the position of my government on that. Second, your future intentions with respect to Saudi Arabia, which you have described. And, last, the safety of American citizens, especially the issue of American citizens' right to leave. As you know, the Americans are very sensitive to the question of losing their right of movement. This includes the Americans in Kuwait, even given the withdrawal [probably a reference to the bogus partial withdrawal announced shortly after the invasion]."

"How can you say there was no withdrawal and then say something different?"

"I saw three convoys advancing from Basra, and I advised Washington of this."

Saddam Hussein: "Our forces took three days to move into Kuwait. As for withdrawal, it cannot be achieved in one day. The withdrawal of our forces has to be based on an international agreement, and we will never allow Kuwait to fall into the hands of another power. If threats against Kuwait escalate, we will add more forces. The nature of our forces will depend on the nature of the threat to Kuwait. When the threat ends, all the forces will withdraw. We do not wish Kuwait to become another Lebanon. I believe that it is not in anyone's interest that the Iraqi army withdraw in a hurry, leaving Kuwait to the warring parties. The provisional government took our advice to form separate militias, and we advised them to be self-sufficient and to use the Popular Army. As for the Americans in Kuwait and Iraq, all Iraqis and foreigners, in both Iraq and Kuwait, are forbidden to travel. Your sources know that our army treated foreigners in a disciplined manner. The communiqué of the Kuwaiti government has allowed foreigners to travel to Iraq where there is safety."

"Can I ask you directly when you are going to allow American citizens, both residents and visitors, to leave?" asked Wilson.

"You mean, when will all foreigners be allowed to leave?"

"I do not permit myself to talk on behalf of others," Wilson replied.

"I wanted to make it clear that this restriction does not apply only to the Americans. In due course we will inform you."

Wilson said: "Please allow me to ask you that you study this question urgently because it is a highly emotional and sensitive issue, both for our government and our people."

"We understand that, and we also understand the humanitarian aspect," Saddam Hussein responded.

Wilson continued: "Finally, I would like to say two things. You have pointed to the good behavior of Iraqi troops, and your Minister and your Vice Minister have also assured me of this, and I think it is expected. Let me draw your attention— this an important point—to the fact that last night the house of the Councillor of the Embassy of Kuwait was broken into by Iraqi soldiers. This contradicts the policy that you have outlined, and I add that it is also a violation of diplomatic immunity. I would not have said this if you had not brought up the matter."

"Yesterday I met with some of our officers and they told me about elements that were breaching security: Asians, Saudis and others. Anyway, if the Iraqi army did this, we would admit it and assure you that it was a mistake, and we would take measures to punish those involved. This behavior is against our policy."

"Last point," said Wilson. "During these difficult days, especially on the safety of the American citizens . . ."

The President interrupted: "Do you plan to attack us, and for that reason you want to remove your citizens?"

"No. But it is my duty to give them the freedom to decide to leave. I personally will stay, and I love life here. I would also like to say that during the crisis the doors were always open to me and to my colleagues in the Foreign Ministry from 8:00 A.M. to 4:00 P.M., and I appreciate that. I appreciate too your wish to meet with me and to reassure me about the fate of our citizens in Kuwait."

"Rest assured," said Saddam Hussein.

"I would like to assure you of my professionalism. Dialogue is the lifeline for diplomats and politicians."

The President replied: "It is natural that you assure me of the good intentions of your colleagues, but you must assure me of your undertaking to carry my letter to President Bush."

"Last time I met a President in Africa," Wilson said, "I asked him to go back to the minutes of the meeting. If you go back through our conversation, you will find that I thanked you a lot."

At 10:00 P.M. (local time) Richard Cheney telephoned the White House on a special line from his hotel in Jeddah. It was then 3:00 P.M. in Washington. Cheney informed George Bush of the Saudi go-ahead, which came with one condition attached: the United States was to postpone a public announcement until the first troops had arrived. Cheney then called Colin Powell. At 4:00 P.M. the President gave the final order for the deployment of American forces. In conversation with Powell, he assigned the troops three objectives: to deter Iraq from any aggressive act; to defend Saudi Arabia; and to strengthen the military capabilities of the Arabian peninsula. The commanding officers had received orders to be in readiness for other missions, but nothing was said about the possibility of an offensive to force Iraq out of Kuwait.

An hour later an F15 fighter squadron took off for Saudi Arabia. Operation Desert Shield had begun. In December 1989 it had taken George Bush nineteen hours to reach a decision about the invasion of Panama; this time it had taken him 115 hours to respond militarily to the invasion of Kuwait.

Margaret Thatcher, on her way home from Colorado, stopped off in Washington, where she was received by George Bush shortly after he had met with NATO Secretary-General Manfred Woerner. In the meantime the result of the vote by the UN Security Council had reached the White House.

Resolution 661 had been passed by thirteen votes, with two abstentions: Cuba and Yemen. The resolution "advocated" the commercial, financial, and military boycott of Iraq. Shortly afterward the aircraft carrier *Saratoga* and the battleship *Wisconsin* left for the Gulf. The United States was reinforcing its naval presence in the region in anticipation of a military blockade designed to back up the UN resolution.

Bush questioned Thatcher at length about her conduct of the Falklands war and the particular difficulties she had had to face.

The same day the White House received first a brief cable, then the full text, of the conversation between Saddam and the chargé d'affaires in Baghdad, Joseph Wilson. Once it had been deciphered, the content of the interview was greeted with little enthusiasm. It is true that Saddam Hussein had stated that he had no intention of invading Saudi Arabia, but there was a great deal of skepticism about the statement. "It's difficult to give any credibility to what he says," said one of Bush's aides, "when he was full of similar assurances just before he invaded Kuwait."

The United Nations Security Council was meeting to adopt Resolution 661, which would impose sanctions on Iraq. But something happened there that gives the impression that while the White House was rejecting Joe Wilson's information about

Saddam Hussein, they were ready to move on a softer path towards the Iraqi leader.

The U.S. Ambassador Thomas Pickering saw the Jordanian Ambassador Abdullah Salah looking depressed. Pickering walked over to him. "Buck up. Get off a message to Amman to send to Baghdad and make them reply. It's not too late to retrieve the situation." He then dictated five points to the Ambassador.

1. There should be a public withdrawal and a statement that specifies the time sequence—for example, by Wednesday we will do such and such. But there's no need to do this overnight.

2. Don't worry about the return of the Emir and his family; this can be handled later.

3. We believe there is merit in your (Saddam Hussein's) position and in the outstanding issues between you and Kuwait, and, while we are not taking a position one way or another, we will do whatever is necessary to develop the institutions, such as mediation, that may be required.

4. We acknowledge your need for an opening to the Gulf, and the issue of access to the islands (Warbah and Bubyan) is one that we could look on favorably.

5. We suggest you call publicly for a UN-sponsored plebiscite providing for Kuwaiti citizens to decide their future.

The Jordanian Ambassador sent off the message that night and was awakened early the next morning by Zaid bin Shaker, Chief of the Royal Court. "It's fascinating," he told the Ambassador, "but is it off the top of Pickering's head or is it a trial balloon from the Administration?"

Ambassador Salah called Pickering to see if this proposal represented administration thinking. Pickering answered: "I don't know for sure, but I'm pretty sure this is close to administration views."

Pickering then called Secretary of State James Baker. Baker said he would get right back to him. Baker called Pickering five minutes later and said, "We can live with this." Pickering then confirmed his conversation with Baker to the Jordanian Ambassador. The message was to have gone through immediately to Saddam Hussein, but there is no confirmation it ever reached him.

8

"A Line Has Been Drawn in the Sand"

When Yasser Arafat and Abu Iyad landed at Jeddah Airport at 7:00 A.M. on August 7, they, like the rest of the world, were unaware of the agreement reached between the Saudi leaders and Washington and of the imminence of Operation Desert Shield.

It was late at night at the military bases on the East Coast of the United States. The troops who would be the first to leave were stationed here, but as yet there were no signs of unusual activity.

The two Palestinian leaders were puzzled by the prevailing mood in King Fahd's palace. They were accustomed to a calm, hushed, rather soporific atmosphere. Now they came upon a veritable hive of activity. A constant stream of cars was arriving at the palace, bringing leading figures of the regime to see the King, while other officials were hurrying busily along the corridors with files in their hands.

Arafat and Abu Iyad were kept waiting for a while until a

colleague of the King came up to them and informed them that Fahd would not be able to receive them until the following day.

"Why all this excitement?" asked Arafat, indicating the unaccustomed bustle.

Fahd's colleague hesitated, then replied, "The American Defense Secretary arrived yesterday at the head of a delegation. He's continuing his talks with the King today."

Arafat was disturbed by the news. Abu Iyad, who was responsible for the security and intelligence services of the PLO, had not been informed of the visit.

The two men also wondered about their schedule. Before they had taken the decision to come to Saudi Arabia to see King Fahd, they had planned to fly to Vienna to attend the funeral of the former Austrian Chancellor, Bruno Kreisky, which was due to take place that day. Although of Jewish origin, Kreisky had always defended the Palestinians. It was now too late to make the journey, as there was no flight that could take them from Jeddah to Vienna in time. They disclosed their disappointment to the King's colleague who had announced the postponement of the meeting. The man listened carefully, then left them for about twenty minutes. When he returned he wore a satisfied smile on his face. "It's all arranged. The King has ordered a plane for you. It's ready to take off now. It'll fly you to Vienna and bring you back to Jeddah this evening."

Meanwhile in Jerusalem the funerals of two murdered young Israelis were giving rise to violent expressions of anti-Arab feeling.

At the headquarters of military intelligence two issues were worrying the experts. By invading Kuwait the Iraqis had laid their hands on a quantity of sophisticated military materiel, largely American in origin, belonging to the Kuwaiti army: materiel similar to that used by Israel's own forces. In addition, "sources" revealed that, in preparing for the invasion, the Iraqi secret services had received a good deal of intelligence from the PLO—intelligence that had come from many Palestinians holding important posts in the Emirate.

In the United States, while several F-15 and F-16 fighter squadrons were taking off for Saudi Arabia, 4,000 men of the 82nd Airborne Division were getting ready to leave.

The first effects of Washington's political pressure were also beginning to be felt. The Saudis closed the pipeline carrying Iraqi oil to the Red Sea ports, and Turkey prohibited the transport of Iraqi oil to its Mediterranean coast.

As a European politician put it, there were two approaches to the problem: "Confrontation or strangulation." George Bush had chosen to play both cards at once. For both to be effective, a broad degree of international coordination and cooperation was required.

Within the closed circle of Bush's colleagues who were in the know there was much lively debate about the best moment at which to announce the massive deployment of troops in the Gulf. Most leaned toward the idea of a television broadcast on Tuesday evening, "before the press has made the operation public." Bush, who was never very comfortable speaking on television, persisted in the rather enigmatic belief that the announcement had to be made "at the right moment, politically and militarily."

In a speech on Iraqi television Saddam Hussein asserted that the occupation of Kuwait had "put an end to a colonial partition" that had separated the poor majority from a wealthy minority.

Having returned from Vienna during the night, Arafat and Abu Iyad were received by King Fahd on the morning of August 8.

Crown Prince Abdullah was also present at the meeting. The first American forces were beginning to arrive on Saudi soil.

For years Arafat had been a master of the art of survival. In taking over the role of mediator, after King Hussein of Jordan had bowed out in discouragement, Arafat thought that he could enhance the prestige of the PLO not only among Arab heads of state but also in the West. He had refused to condemn the invasion of Kuwait and considered this a trump card that allowed him to remain in close contact with Saddam Hussein.

But, far from being a strength, his refusal had, in fact, weakened his position. Syria's Hafez El Assad despised him; Egypt's President Mubarak mistrusted him; and the Gulf states had denounced his stand. Only Saudi Arabia, which was also his main financial backer, maintained a moderate attitude toward the PLO.

Before arriving in Riyadh Arafat and Abu Iyad had considered the possible financial consequences of the crisis for their organization. Some trusted advisers had even uttered the word "bankruptcy." If the 400,000 Palestinians working in the Gulf lost their jobs, and if the kingdoms of the reign rescinded their grants, the PLO would find itself virtually without resources. Arafat had asked for a plan to be drawn up that would take into account a cut of 35 percent in the annual budget of $1 billion. He had come to Jeddah not only to negotiate but also to beg.

King Fahd, who was usually level-headed, surprised his guests by the violence of his attack on the Al Sabahs, the former Kuwaiti ruling family who had taken refuge on his soil. "I have a lot of criticisms to make of them," said Fahd, in a rage. "They didn't pay their debts. They are largely responsible for this crisis."

The King then discussed with the Palestinian leaders a plan for withdrawal from Kuwait that could be presented to Saddam

Hussein. It allowed for the Iraqis to withdraw to the disputed border area where the oilfields were located but to remain on the two islands that gave them access to the Gulf.

"Would you be prepared to meet the Iraqi leader, Your Majesty?"

Fahd glanced at Crown Prince Abdullah, then replied: "Yes, if he abides by these conditions." He also agreed to give money to Iraq. Throughout the interview he spoke of Saddam Hussein "in a very proper manner."

The conversation took a turn that was unpleasant for the two Palestinians when the question of the PLO's finances was raised. Abdullah, whose opinions were more cut and dried than those of Fahd, lost his temper. "You Palestinians seem to be completely unaware of everything the Kuwaitis have done for you. You've never done anything in return for the trust and the help they've given you."

The exchange grew increasingly heated until Fahd ordered them all to stop.

At 4:00 A.M. George Bush left his apartments for the Situation Room. There, together with Brent Scowcroft, he supervised the departure of the troops. At 6:00 A.M., as he was returning to the Oval Office, he passed a journalist accredited to the White House and told him to keep listening to the radio. At 9:00 A.M. he received the press in his office and announced the operation. At midday he held a press conference, at which he declared: "A line has been drawn in the sand." In the evening he addressed the nation on television.

It was a task he hated. Appearing grave and tense, he stated: "There comes a time in the life of a nation when we are called to find out who we are and what we believe in. Today, as your President, I'm asking for your support for a decision I have taken to allow us to stand firm for what is right and to condemn what is bad." Bush made it clear that the mission of the American forces was a purely defensive one. He listed four objectives: Iraq's immediate and unconditional withdrawal from Kuwait; the restoration of the legitimate government of the Emirate; the security of the Gulf region, especially its oil reserves; and the protection of American lives.

Immediately after the President's broadcast the Revolution Command Council in Baghdad issued a communiqué announcing the "annexation of Kuwait." The move was described as a "permanent union."

In the Saudi desert, not far from the city of Dharan where the huge oil consortium ARAMCO had its headquarters, the first troops were being deployed. According to Pentagon sources, 50,000 men would be in place by the end of the month.

The Arab world was making a last desperate attempt to settle the crisis. Since the previous day Hosni Mubarak had been contacting all the leaders in the region to organize a summit in Cairo on August 10.

Meanwhile the government in Baghdad was taking steps to sever its remaining ties with the outside world. On August 9, twenty-four hours after the announcement of the annexation, Iraq decided to close its borders and to hold all foreigners present on its territory "for security reasons," thereby making 3 million people hostages.

It was also declared that all foreign embassies in Kuwait would have to close by August 24. At the same time the international press was given special treatment. Journalists were free to enter and leave, and the American TV networks were particularly favored.

Faced with both the blockade and the military response, Iraqi officials replied: "We can live without Pepsi, without Macintosh computers and without whisky." They omitted to mention that Iraq suffered from a serious shortage of cereal crops and imported, among other things, three-quarters of its wheat, as well as large amounts of rice, sugar, and meat. The regime had, in fact, been stocking up in anticipation of the crisis.

Suddenly Saddam Hussein had become strangely absent from the country he had shaped. His portrait was everywhere—in the streets, on the sides of monuments, on public buildings. He had remade every truth, bent every reality to his wishes. Baghdad's equivalent of the Arc de Triomphe was called "the Hands of Victory": a monument thirty feet high in the form of two crossed swords held by two giant bronze forearms. The design reproduced the coat of arms that Saddam Hussein had devised for himself and symbolized Iraq's victory over Iran—a victory that had never happened. But the Iraqi people had not protested. The secret police were too vigilant for that. As a diplomat put it, "only snatches of outer reality" reached the country. Saddam had made his country in his own image: like him, it was ignorant of the outside world and had a taste for isolation.

At this point, in early August, nobody had seen the Iraqi leader for days. Anti-aircraft defenses had been strengthened around the presidential palace, but he was seldom there. Afraid of bombs and of assassination attempts, he liked to change residences every six hours and spent most of his time in his bunker. He had long been accustomed to acting with no other purpose in mind than to stay alive. Now, as he well knew, he was playing the most dangerous game of his career.

He had burned all his bridges. In this period of international condemnation no foreign visitors were in a hurry to come to Baghdad, except for Yasser Arafat and Abu Iyad on their continuing pilgrimage in search of peace.

Saddam Hussein came out of hiding to meet them. He appeared neither surprised nor bothered by the massive campaign mobilized against him. Things had become much more complicated since the last time Saddam and Arafat had met: the annexation of Kuwait had been announced, and American troops were arriving in Saudi Arabia. The meeting was to last almost three hours.

Arafat and Abu Iyad tried to persuade Saddam to attend the Cairo summit the next day. Saddam refused to go if the Emir of Kuwait was planning to attend. Try as they might, the Palestinians could not get him to yield on this point. "The monarchy and its representatives have simply ceased to exist," he said, angrily: it was the one moment in the conversation when he lost his composure.

The Palestinians then proposed another plan. Arafat would go to Cairo and persuade the leaders of five key countries taking part in the summit to visit Baghdad for negotiations. The summit would adjourn until they returned. It was a complex and risky proposal that could succeed, as Arafat and Iyad well knew, only if they managed to convince those five heads of state as soon as they arrived in Cairo. But Saddam Hussein agreed to the idea.

When the strictly diplomatic part of the meeting was over, Saddam Hussein did not let the two men go but continued talking. In a calm, resolute tone he spoke of the huge, apocalyptic conflagration he could provoke in the region. There was no bombast in his manner. He was clear and precise, like a bomb expert laying a charge and selecting the exact moment for the explosion.

He talked about the possibility of a war with the United States. "It's obvious that as soon as I'm attacked, I'll attack Israel. Israeli involvement in the conflict will change everyone's attitude in the Arab world, and the aggression against Iraq will be seen as an American–Zionist plot. Several countries that are currently supporting the United States, especially Egypt and Syria, will change their minds when they see that Israel is involved in the war."

Later in the conversation he explained: "I'm in the process of strengthening the military infrastructure of Kuwait. There'll be four lines of defense, including two to protect Kuwait City, that the foreign forces will have to break through if they want to retake Kuwait. Even if the United States has air superiority, my troops will inflict great losses on the invading forces."

The third aspect of his plan concerned Saudi Arabia: "A group has been formed, composed of Iraqis and Saudis, ready to launch terrorist attacks against American troops stationed on Saudi territory.

"If war breaks out," he concluded, "there'll be fighting within Saudi Arabia. In the past five years dozens of arms, mostly of Polish or Czech manufacture, have been smuggled across the border from Yemen. They are now in the hands of tribesmen hostile to the Saudi royal family."

Some hundreds of miles away, in Ankara, President Ozal found himself in a difficult position. He had Secretary of State James Baker with him. Baker thanked him for shutting the pipeline that carried oil from Iraq and added, "That isn't the main purpose of our talks. . . ." Ozal listened carefully. He was starting to feel worried. "The important thing is to consider how and under what conditions your military bases might be used."

Ozal's reply was full of vague generalities: "Turkey has had close ties with the West since the Republic was proclaimed in 1923, but we also have a traditional historical relationship with the Arab and Islamic world."

"That's true," Baker concurred. "The present crisis demonstrates the strategic importance of your country and its role within NATO. That's why we'd like to know if we could use your bases."

"In what context, Mr. Secretary of State?"

"There are several options," replied Baker. "The most drastic would, of course, be an offensive against Iraq."

Ozal gave an embarrassed smile. "That's a very delicate point. Your forces can use our bases in the context of regular NATO exercises, but the possibility you envisage . . ."

"Of course," Baker cut in, "any move will first be submitted to your government for approval."

"I think we could agree in the following way. We'll accede to your demands if military action becomes . . ."

"Necessary?" Baker ventured.

Ozal shook his head. "No, I'd prefer the word 'unavoidable.' "

Baker assented and went on to talk of the possibility that Turkey might participate in the multinational force now in place to defend Saudi Arabia. Ozal, who had been joined by his Foreign Minister, did not seem enthusiastic. "It's a possibility to be considered."

"In any case," said Baker, amiably, "that's a question that really has to be settled between Turkey and Saudi Arabia and not between Turkey and the United States."

Shortly afterward Turkey's leaders brought up the question of the financial sacrifices incurred by their country in joining in sanctions against Iraq. Questioned by Baker, they estimated their losses at nearly $6 billion. The Secretary of State promised American assistance and added, "The legitimate government of Kuwait, now in exile, offers to help in reducing the losses incurred by Turkey."

In Amman King Hussein was getting ready to fly to Cairo for the following day's summit. For the journey he had chosen a Royal Jordanian Airlines Airbus called *Baghdad*. He rejected the suggestion by his aides that the name be painted over. He was hoping, in the course of the summit, to propose the creation of a committee of arbitration, composed of Arab heads of state, and to ask the Gulf states to support a petition aimed at reducing the American military presence in the region.

For Washington the summit was an event of great importance. The U.S. administration was hoping that a majority of UN member countries would vote to send contingents to the multinational force.

On August 7, on his way back from his talks in Saudi Arabia, Cheney had made a stop in Cairo, where he had asked Hosni Mubarak to send troops on to Saudi soil. Although he was to deny it later, the Egyptian President agreed "on condition that other Arab countries also give their agreement." No sooner had Cheney's Boeing left Cairo and begun to fly over the Mediterranean than the Defense Secretary received a call from George Bush. "Dick," said the President, "I'd like you to go to Morocco to meet King Hassan." The request was so unexpected that the flight plan and maps showing the route to Rabat Airport had to be faxed immediately to the crew of Cheney's plane. The interview with the King proved fruitless. The King refused to send troops, and when Mubarak learned of his position he in turn went back on his decision.

The Arab regimes were showing themselves to be weak and vulnerable, less inclined to stand firm than to seek compromise. In the past most summits had been distinguished by a reluctance to reach any decision on the questions tackled. But this time the Arab countries had their backs to the wall and were unable to conceal their equivocation.

The maneuvering in Cairo began on August 9, while Arafat was still in Baghdad trying to convince Saddam Hussein to go to the Egyptian capital.

Gaddafi had been the first to arrive, at about 9:00 P.M. on August 8. The Iraqi delegation arrived at about 4:00 A.M. the next day on board a plane named after Saladin, the legendary hero whose exploits held such fascination for Saddam Hussein. The delegation, which consisted of three men—Deputy Prime Minister Saddoum Hammadi, Foreign Minister Tariq Aziz, and Taha Yassin Ramadan, head of the Popular Army—went immediately to the Meridian, a hotel built in the middle of the Nile, where most of the delegations were being accommodated.

Mubarak wanted to take advantage of the twenty-four hours before the summit officially opened to try to get the Iraqis to soften their position. He received the Iraqi delegation in his residence that morning for talks that lasted more than three hours. The effort was in vain. Neither side would budge. Saddoun Hammadi and Ramadan wanted to discuss the blockade and the American military presence. The first they described as "an act of piracy," the second as "an act of war."

Mubarak had two dreams: that Egypt should once again become the "center of gravity" of the Arab world, and that the United States, with whom he was in negotiation, should write off his $7.1 billion worth of military debts. He hoped that the results of the Cairo summit would allow his dreams to become a reality.

In fact, as the hours wore on, the situation would become ever more strained—even, occasionally, tragicomic.

This was the first public appearance, since the beginning of their exile, of the former rulers of Kuwait, who were still the legitimate recognized government of that country. The Emir had been very reluctant to make the journey, and it had taken the combined pressure of the Saudis and the Americans, infuriated by his indecision, to persuade him to come to Cairo. He had specified that he would attend only the opening session on August 10 and then return to Saudi Arabia. He struck everyone present as being "in a state of shock."

The Iraqi and Kuwaiti delegations were brought together at an informal meeting. Tariq Aziz entered the room without so much as a glance at the Al Sabahs, especially Foreign Minister Sheikh Sabah Al Ahmad. All the Kuwaitis were wearing bulletproof vests.

Tariq Aziz addressed the meeting: "I protest against the presence here of American puppets."

Sheikh Sabah Al Ahmad rose furiously to his feet. "You've violated every international law and—"

"Shut up!" Aziz cut him off. His voice was ice-cold. "You're nothing but an American mercenary who's been working for the CIA for years."

The Sheikh, enraged beyond measure, tried to rise again but felt dizzy and fell back on to his seat, unconscious.

Tariq Aziz persisted: "Since the Al Sabahs fled, Kuwait has been free!"

Several hours later the confrontation continued, this time at a hotel restaurant. Iraqis and Kuwaitis traded insults, and at one point Ramadan hurled a dish on to the floor in front of Sheikh Saad, who rose and then collapsed. Five minutes later he revived and left the room.

The Cairo summit was getting under way in a grim atmosphere.

The plenary session began at 2:30 P.M. on August 10. Mubarak presided. He did his best to put on a good front, greeting each head of state with a smile, holding the hands of some for a chat, as was the custom. Perhaps the worst could be avoided after all.

But at this "last-chance summit" the worst was what, in fact, happened.

At Mubarak's side, silent and reduced to a walk-on role, sat Chadli Klibi, Secretary General of the Arab League. Fourteen heads of state and monarchs, five government delegations, and PLO chief Yasser Arafat were present. Tunisia was not represented.

Since their arrival the Saudi delegates had been conspicuously avoiding their Iraqi counterparts. In a break with alphabetical order, the delegation from Qatar had been placed between Iraq and Kuwait in order to avoid another confrontation.

Mubarak demanded "the withdrawal of all Iraqi forces from Kuwait, respect for the rights of the Kuwaiti people, and the restoration of the legitimate government that existed before the invasion." But he also implicitly criticized the Saudi agreement to accept American troops.

Fahd was furious. He would later say to one of his peers, "I took that decision because the satellite photos the Americans showed me proved that the Iraqi threat was a real one and also because I trust George Bush. I've known him for years, since the time when I was Interior Minister and he was Director of the CIA."

Mubarak concluded his speech by saying, "The Arab of the twenty-first century must not be a weak man, lost in the darkness of ignorance and failure. The Arab nation must not be 'the sick man of the century.'" Emir Jaber and Taha Yassin Ramadan—who had finally agreed to leave his gun at the door—clapped in unison. It was to be the one moment of unanimity.

The session was adjourned, and all the participants attended

Friday prayers in the mosque that had been set up inside the Palace of Congress.

At 3:30 P.M. the closed session began. It would last for five hours, and the leader of one of the delegations would describe it as "a disaster for Arab unity."

Yasser Arafat later claimed that when he took his seat, he was surprised to find on the table the text of a final communiqué—written in English and translated into Arabic. This fact was confirmed by four other delegations.

The leaders of the PLO were beginning to realize just how isolated they were. Many heads of state did not acknowledge their greetings or conspicuously turned away to avoid having to speak to them. The Palestinians were paying the price for supporting Saddam Hussein. Even the King of Jordan, who admitted that he had underestimated the scale of Western reaction, had begun to distance himself from the Iraqi leader. He had recognized the Kuwaiti government in exile and had agreed to take part in UN sanctions. Shortly afterward the Jordanian port of Aqaba, an unloading point for many goods destined for Iraq, would be closed.

Many delegates were surprised by the way Mubarak conducted the debate. First, the Iraqi delegation attacked the former government of Kuwait violently. Then when Arafat, after a long and somewhat confused preamble, tried to put forward his plan Mubarak cried, impatiently: "Keep to the agenda. We don't have much time."

"I propose," Arafat continued, "that five heads of state, those of Jordan, Yemen, Algeria, Egypt, and Palestine, form a committee of mediation and go to Baghdad in the next few hours."

"I'm certainly not going to make a journey like that," Mubarak cut in angrily. "Saddam Hussein has betrayed my trust. Let's get on with the voting, Abu."

"But I haven't had a chance to speak!" exclaimed Arafat in astonishment.

Another delegate intervened: "Let's not forget we're brothers."

"Yes, we are," replied Mubarak, "but let's get on with the voting."

Several countries—the Gulf states, Egypt, Syria, Morocco, and Saudi Arabia—seemed to have decided already to support the resolution that had been placed on each delegation's table before the session started. The seven-point resolution, which many thought had been drawn up, or at least inspired, by the Americans, rejected the annexation of Kuwait, supported the UN sanctions and embargo against Iraq, and called for the formation of Arab expeditionary forces that would be sent to Saudi Arabia. Twelve of the twenty-one members of the Arab League voted in favor of the resolution; three—Iraq, Libya, and the PLO—voted against; others, such as Algeria and Yemen, abstained; while Jordan did not even take part in the voting—King Hussein remained stiffly in his seat. The deployment of troops and the creation of an Arab peace-keeping force were being undertaken in an atmosphere of sorrow and confusion.

"It's a mistake, a terrible mistake," cried Arafat in the corridors immediately after the vote. "If a delegation had gone to Baghdad, it could have reached a solution that would have settled the Gulf crisis."

After the vote Colonel Gaddafi of Libya remained behind. The only other person in the room was Chadli Klibli. The Libyan leader started shouting at him, "What you did was illegal. That is not the way the Arab League solves problems." He went on shouting until Klibi left the room and went up to his suite. About ten minutes later a Libyan delegation arrived at his door. Its members told Klibi that they had come to apologize for

Gaddafi's behavior. "He wasn't angry with you," they said. "He was angry with Mubarak."

The confrontation continued the following day. Mubarak and Syria's Hafez El Assad, who had been allies during the summit, were leaving for Alexandria and invited Gaddafi to join them. Once they were in private Mubarak went up to Gaddafi, pointing threateningly with his finger, as Assad looked on impassively. "How can you agree with the occupation of Kuwait? Be careful. If you continue like this, I'll occupy your country tomorrow and nobody will say a word."

The Arab decision to create an international contingent parallel with the American forces had two contradictory objectives: to satisfy the Americans, as some wanted, and to prevent Western intervention in the region. Mubarak had implicitly stated this mistrust of foreign influence during the summit when he had said, "The choice for us is clear: an Arab action that preserves our best interests or foreign intervention over which we have no authority and no control."

The Arab leaders who had voted in favor of sending troops feared the reaction of public opinion in their countries. There was a tradition that if a nation whose religion was Islam allowed infidels to fight on its soil, all the other Islamic countries had to turn against the renegade.

Nobody was under any illusion. The imminent confrontation would be essentially a duel between Iraq and the United States, the nations of the Arab world merely acting as seconds.

Saddam Hussein was well aware of the fact. While the stormy proceedings were continuing in Cairo, Saddam, in a televised speech read by a presenter who was almost his double, made what amounted to a call for "a holy war against the United States and the corrupt Arab leaders." He claimed that Mecca, the birthplace of the Prophet Mohammed, would be defiled by the arrival of American troops.

In Washington Saddam's call was interpreted by the CIA as incitement to overthrow the regime of King Fahd. CIA Director William Webster spoke about it with President Bush, who had just arrived, late in the afternoon, at his residence in Kennebunkport, Maine, where he was planning to spend a few days' vacation. Something else was worrying Webster. That same day, at the instigation of the Muslim Brotherhood, thousands of people had demonstrated their support for Saddam Hussein in the streets of Amman. More than 40,000 Jordanians had already volunteered to fight on the Iraqi side. The risks of a conflagration were increasing.

CIA analysts had been evaluating carefully the weaknesses of several of the Allied nations. That of Jordan was the most obvious, although, as one expert put it, King Hussein "had changed his skin a million times in order to survive." His throne had never seemed so threatened. The economic blockade against Iraq, which he had agreed to respect, would entail a huge loss of revenue for his country, which could ill afford it. In addition, if Saddam Hussein decided to attack Israel, Jordan would be in the front line. Egypt's position was not much better. Mubarak had declared: "When Saddam Hussein lied to me, forty million Egyptians felt insulted," but he could not ignore the fact that 1.5 million Egyptians worked in Iraq and a further 150,000 in Kuwait. If they were expelled, the already critical state of the Egyptian economy would worsen. Nor did the experts express much enthusiasm about the participation of Syria, a country that, just a short time before, had been described by the Americans as a "terrorist state." "Assad is going to try to get as much as he can from us," one declared. The Lebanese affair would prove how right he was.

Bush's conversation with Webster took place in the brightly colored, simply furnished living room of the house at Kennebunkport. Built of wood and located near the sea and a golf course, the house had for many years been the favorite retreat of Bush and his family. It had been built by his grandfather, a polo player of repute.

Webster went on to speak of Saudi Arabia. The kingdom had never been so rich or so exposed. The pressure on oil prices would allow the country to double its revenue: more than $95 billion the following year. But there was other information that was more worrying. Fahd was being heavily criticized within the royal family for the go-ahead he had given the Americans, and in the holy places of Mecca and Medina recordings of radical preachers were beginning to circulate, "passing harsh judgments on the ruling family." In the war of words the Iraqis were stressing the issue of the American presence, which, they said, would lead to "an orgy of sex and alcohol."

After this conversation George Bush phoned the Pentagon and spoke to Richard Cheney and Colin Powell. They decided to increase the number of "special forces" to be sent into the field. These consisted of several hundred men belonging to SEAL units of the Navy and the Delta force attached to the land army. Their mission was to protect the oilfields against terrorist attack and to hold themselves in readiness for possible operations to save American "hostages"—although the word had not yet been uttered. It was also decided that several units would be assigned to guard the leading members of the Saudi royal family.

On the ground in Saudi Arabia Lieutenant General Charles Horner was coordinating the arrival of the airborne forces. By the end of the week more than 200 fighter aircraft would be at the Saudi bases, together with 100 support planes. Fifty B-52 bombers were waiting on the island of Diego Garcia, ready, as one officer put it, "to spread a carpet of bombs" on Iraqi military targets. Fourteen F-111 fighter-bombers were stationed at bases in Turkey. In all the Pentagon was expecting the arrival of 600 planes to counter the 500 planes possessed by the Iraqis, of which only about 100—Mig-23s and Mirage F-1s—could be considered a serious threat.

From his headquarters in Riyadh General Norman Schwarzkopf was supervising every detail of the operation. The commander-in-chief of the American forces, now nicknamed "the Desert Bear" by analogy with Rommel, had a permanent hotline to Colin Powell in Washington. The two men spoke to each other every day. According to Schwarzkopf, "The forces we have on the ground have both defensive and offensive capabilities."

The Pentagon was operating what amounted to an airlift to Saudi Arabia. Every five minutes a giant C-141 landed at a Saudi base. More than 450,000 tons of materiel would be delivered in this way. Besides military parts, the mountains of crates contained products as diverse as 168,000 sets of equipment designed to protect the troops against chemical weapons and 150,000 bottles of suntan lotion. Within the army only Powell, Schwarzkopf, and their closest colleagues knew that this massive effort would end with the presence of 250,000 soldiers in the Saudi desert. Never since the Vietnam war had the United States carried out such a deployment of forces or given such an impressive display of its military might.

Every morning, while his troops were continuing to leave for the desert, Bush went for a relaxing round of golf on the course at Kennebunkport. Occasionally he would break off his game to phone his colleagues in Washington or a leader somewhere in the world. An assistant was constantly at his side carrying a portable phone that allowed him to call any spot on the globe.

Since the beginning of the crisis Bush had shed the reputation of a "wimp" that had previously pursued him. Now he was more like a resolute sheriff, ordering the Israelis to remain calm and discreet, telling the Japanese to make a firmer commitment than a mere financial contribution, making it clear to the Chinese and the Soviets that now they had a unique opportunity to become part of the international community, gaining the support of his European allies and most of the Arab countries.

Bush's character was more complex than it had appeared at first. An East Coast patrician and a lover of classical music, courtly in his speech and restrained in his manner, he was also a man who had made his fortune in the Texas oil business, a "wild-money man," ruthless in his dealings and crazy about country music.

His "telephone diplomacy," his endless conversations with world leaders, were other examples of this duality. On the one hand, he criticized King Hussein harshly for his equivocal position and his thinly disguised support for Baghdad. The King, impressed by his bluntness, reminded Bush that he had always been a faithful ally of the United States. "We must talk about that," replied Bush dryly. Hussein offered to come to the United States to meet the President in a few days' time, after a visit to Baghdad to see Saddam, from whom he expected concessions. "I'm skeptical," was Bush's verdict.

On the other hand, he once stayed up until 2:30 in the morning to call François Mitterrand in Paris, where it was then 8:30, for fear of waking him. And his first anxious words were: "Mr. President, I hope I'm not disturbing you by calling you so early."

———

In the waiting game that was now under way in the desert the strengths and weaknesses of the Iraqi army had been considered at length. In the eyes of the American experts it was almost a "Warsaw Pact army," equipped largely with Soviet materiel and trained along the lines of the Red Army. Attacks were launched by Soviet T-72 and T-62 tanks and preceded by barrage fire from 122-mm and 152-mm guns. Aerial defense was handled by batteries of mobile SAM missiles and ZSU-23 anti-aircraft radar equipment. The Iraqi navy was almost non-existent; a number of Iraq's 5,500 tanks were old models; and its air force was not, for the most part, equipped with technology that would allow it to conduct aerial combat efficiently.

But a ground war with the main aim of retaking Kuwait risked being very costly in terms of human lives. The estimates that the Pentagon and the chiefs of staff had drawn up at Bush's request, and that had not yet been passed on to him, put the number of dead at between 20,000 and 30,000, of whom 10,000 might die in the first days of fighting. It was an enormous human and political price to pay.

The American administration was hoping that the size of the forces deployed and the effectiveness of the blockade would made Saddam Hussein change his tune. Iraq was no longer able to export its oil—its one source of revenue—or to import anything, even food.

In order to evaluate the impact of sanctions, the CIA and the other intelligence agencies were coordinating their intelligence-gathering operations. The first element was the photographs taken by spy satellites, which could show with precision all civilian and military movements and the developing situation in the field. This activity was the responsibility of the NSA, which also had top-secret listening stations in Turkey. The stations could pick up most phone calls made in Iraq, and the details could then be transmitted immediately to the United States, where translators and linguists could evaluate, from the words used and the tone of voice, the morale of the population, its potential discontent, and the first signs of economic hardship. A huge computer program had been set in motion at CIA headquarters in Langley to integrate all existing data—even such things as an increase in taxi fares—that might reveal a rise in the cost of living, higher fuel prices, and perhaps difficulty in obtaining spare parts.

At the same time a number of "psychological guerrilla warfare" operations were set in motion. They were coordinated within the Deputies Committee—which grouped the deputies of the principal departments—by Robert Gates, ex-CIA number-two man and now Deputy Director of the National Security Council. One of the objectives was to counter Iraqi propaganda. As one of the participants confessed: "We all remember Vietnam, when we lost the war politically."

The Voice of America was now broadcasting to Iraq twenty-four hours a day, although there was one snag: the lack of Arab presenters with an Iraqi accent. Specialists from the Fourth Psychological Operations Group, based at Fort Bragg, North Carolina, were getting ready to leave for Saudi Arabia to implement a disinformation scheme that would undermine the morale of the Iraqi troops massed on the other side of the border—for example, by making them believe that the water in the desert wells was poisoned.

Strong psychological pressure was exerted on Iraq to stress American determination. Soldiers were photographed being trained to carry out house-to-house searches, a task that would fall to them if Kuwait City were retaken.

Robert Gates's group had drawn up a long top-secret memo listing "dos and don'ts." It was intended for all civilian and military officials directly involved in the crisis and constituted a code of conduct, describing, for example, which public statements to make and which to avoid.

A spectacular blunder was made by the head of the Air Force, General Dugan. In an interview he told journalists that a plan to bomb Baghdad existed and that Israel would help the Air Force to select the targets. Dugan was immediately dismissed by Bush. His statement had caused great embarrassment. He had disregarded one of the most important "don'ts" in the famous memo: never mention any form of coooperation with Israel.

In Jerusalem the Israeli leaders were worried. They had received information from the intelligence services that an air attack on the nuclear plant at Dimona, in the Negev desert, was being planned. The threat was taken sufficiently seriously for Hawk missiles to be transferred from the Jordanian border to the nuclear plant to strengthen its existing defense system. The possibility of evacuating the nearby town was even considered.

On August 12, in a speech broadcast on radio and television, Saddam Hussein suggested a comprehensive settlement in the Middle East. He stated that withdrawal from Kuwait could not be considered without also discussing the Syrian presence in Lebanon and the Israeli presence in the Occupied Territories. He called, in fact, for "the immediate and unconditional withdrawal of Israeli troops." Bush responded immediately by calling for "the immediate and unconditional withdrawal of the occupation troops from Kuwait."

The American response did not greatly reassure Israel's Prime Minister Shamir. In his view, Saddam was "trying to weaken the alliance against him." On the West Bank and in Gaza the Palestinians greeted the Iraqi leader's statement enthusiastically. At the regular Sunday meeting of the Israeli cabinet much of the agenda was given over to the Gulf crisis. Defense Secretary Moshe Arens, Chief of Staff Dan Shomron, and Ammon Sharak, head of military intelligence, all spoke at length.

On Monday, August 13, King Hussein arrived in Baghdad. He was due to leave again two days later for Washington, where he hoped to be able to meet George Bush with a message from Saddam Hussein or the draft of a peace plan. Contrary to all logic, the King apparently still believed in an Arab solution. The United States and, since the Cairo summit, the majority of the members of the Arab League had come out against the idea. His country was plunging into economic difficulties, and both Washington and Riyadh now mistrusted him. Several Arab countries had already expelled their Jordanian residents, and information had reached the King that Saudi Arabia, until now his third most important commercial partner, was about to stop buying Jordanian goods.

"Every day that passes," he confessed, "brings us closer to war, and those who claim that an Arab solution is a dead letter forget that it was feasible during the first week of the crisis until the Americans put a stop to it."

The King also knew that he would have to face the hostility of the U.S. Congress, and he had had a letter drafted, one copy of which would go to each of the Senators and Representatives, in which he carefully explained his country's position.

When he emerged from his talks with Saddam Hussein, his face was set and he would not utter a word. His brother, Prince Hassan, revealed that the meeting had been a failure.

On August 14 George Bush briefly interrupted his vacation to return to Washington. Sixty thousand soldiers, sailors, and airmen had already been deployed in Saudi Arabia, and a further 50,000 were expected in the next few days. The Pentagon had assessed the cost of Operation Desert Shield at $10 million a day.

On the morning of August 15 Bush met the leaders of Congress. The President had the authority to call up 120,000 reservists, without needing the approval of Congress, for 180 days. He was trying to maintain the same consensus internally as he had managed to obtain internationally. But, as some of his advisers said, "It'll be easier to get the UN to agree than Congress." And one of them added, "It's true we've promised to consult Congress if there's a war. In other words, we'll phone them just after the first bombs have been dropped."

That day Saddam Hussein's latest initiative had been made public.

In a letter to Iran's President Rafsanjani the Iraqi leader offered peace to the country that until now had been his implacable enemy. He stated that he was abandoning all claims to the border area and announced the withdrawal of Iraqi troops stationed there, starting on August 17. They would be sent to Kuwait and the Saudi border. Finally Saddam agreed to release the 19,000 Iranian prisoners of war he was still holding.

In a few lines Saddam Hussein had wiped out the memory of hundreds of thousands of Iraqi dead and of a conflict considered the deadliest since the Second World War. He had proved once again his skill as a tactician.

The Iraqi withdrawal from the Shatt al-Arab could easily be explained. Thanks to his annexation of Kuwait, Saddam Hussein now had broad access to the Gulf.

In fact, the term "annexation" was almost inappropriate. What had happened was that Kuwait had been absorbed into a greater Iraq. The Western secret services had been wondering for some time about the exact identity of a Colonel Ali who had been described as the leader of the group of "young revolutionaries" that had seized power provisionally in Kuwait City. There was no Colonel Ali in the Kuwaiti army. Further investigation revealed that the man was Saddam Hussein's son-in-law, Ali Hassan Al Majid.

In addition to the 430,000 troops and 3,500 tanks deployed in the region, 7,000 members of the secret police, the Mukhabarat, had been sent to Kuwait. Their objective was to crush the growing resistance movements. The capital had been divided into zones, with numerous checkpoints. Houses were searched, and anyone found in possession of pamphlets or newspapers issued by the underground resistance was immediately executed. Bank records were carefuly checked to identify those officials and civil servants who were paid by checks from government agencies. Schools and police stations were turned into interrogation centers.

Iraqi maps had been redrawn. Kuwait was now shown as the nineteenth province of Iraq. Kuwait City had been renamed Kathima; Iraqi license plates had been affixed to vehicles; and portraits and statues of Saddam Hussein were erected in the streets and squares. As a colleague of the Iraqi leader put it: "Kuwait has been swallowed up in the depths of history and has disappeared from geography."

The Iraqis had seized the wealth of Kuwait. The occupation troops pillaged a little, the leaders on a large scale. One car dealer lost 14,000 brand-new Chevrolets and Oldsmobiles in just a few hours; they were dispatched to Baghdad. Colleagues of several ministers visited the former Emirate with the sole purpose of stocking up on luxury goods. Saddam had not been able to get his hands on the huge Kuwaiti assets that had been frozen in the first hours after the invasion, but special convoys had transported $3 billion in foreign currency and $1 billion in

PIERRE SALINGER WITH ERIC LAURENT

gold from Kuwait City to Baghdad—money stolen from the central bank and the many financial institutions in the country.

On August 16 Saddam Hussein threatened to intern all American and British residents in Kuwait and ordered them to assemble at a hotel. He also threatened to send American soldiers back home "in coffins."

King Hussein arrived that morning in Kennebunkport to meet with President Bush. His friendship with the American President seemed to be deteriorating as the image was spreading that he was becoming an ally of Saddam Hussein. The press indicated that the King was bringing a private message from Saddam Hussein to President Bush. But that was not true. One of the things he wanted to do was to have the President understand the massive efforts he had made to solve the crisis in the first few days. He explained to the President that Saddam Hussein had been ready to withdraw from Kuwait but that he was now taking a much harder position, since U.S. and other troops were being deployed on Saudi Arabian soil. The President answered, "We're there to protect Saudi Arabia against aggression and nothing more. And we'll withdraw when they request." Although they had come to no agreement, the King left his meeting encouraged that President Bush was solely in a defensive mood and that a diplomatic solution was still possible.

The following day the Iraqi government announced that all Westerners under its control would be transferred to strategic civilian and military sites and kept there as long as the threat of war remained. The UN Security Council asked Secretary General Pérez de Cuéllar to act to obtain the release of the foreigners. Meanwhile thirty Iraqi divisions were leaving the Iranian border to join the 150,000 men already in Kuwait.

On August 17 James Baker left Washington for a few days' vacation at his ranch in Wyoming. He was still in daily contact with Eduard Shevardnadze in Moscow. At Bush's suggestion, Baker asked Shevardnadze to support a UN resolution that would permit the use of force to implement the embargo. A game of deception was beginning. The Soviets were dragging their feet, still believing in the possibility of a negotiated solution, while for the Americans time was running out.

On August 20 Iraq's Deputy Prime Minister Saddoum Hammadi was received in Moscow by Soviet officials, who demanded an unconditional withdrawal from Kuwait and the release of all foreigners. Hammadi returned to Baghdad the following day, and Shevardnadze immediately called Baker.

"Wait forty-eight hours before you have a resolution voted on at the UN. The Iraqi Deputy Prime Minister may manage to convince Saddam Hussein."

"And if he fails, will you be on our side in two days' time?"

"I'll confirm that as soon as possible."

The next day Shevardnadze called Baker late in the afternoon. "Jim, we need more time."

"How long?"

"Five days, until August 27."

Baker paused, then said, "That seems too long to me. I have to discuss it with the President."

Baker called Bush. Having returned from his residence in Maine on August 19, he had gone the next day to Baltimore where, in a speech to a veterans' association, he had for the first time described the foreigners detained in Iraq and Kuwait as "hostages." It is a word that has carried an enormous emotional and political charge in the United States since the 1980 Tehran hostage crisis. Bush seemed irritated by the Soviet procrastination and asked Baker to get a shorter postponement.

Baker called Moscow back and said to Shevardnadze, "Hard

to accede to your request. We're under a lot of pressure, especially from the Pentagon, who want to be able to use force to implement the embargo without waiting for UN backing."

Shevardnadze sighed. "I know. We have the same problem with our military. They think we're making a mistake in supporting you. According to them, you have only one objective: to establish a permanent military presence in the Middle East. But to get back to the question of the UN, what are you proposing?"

"To have a resolution passed on the twenty-fourth."

"All right."

"But we will have your support, won't we?"

Shevardnadze's reply was vague. Nevertheless, the following day, August 23, the Soviet chargé d'affaires in Washington, Sergei Shetverikov, presented himself at the State Department. As a token of their good faith, the Soviets had asked him to pass on to the Americans the full text of a message from Gorbachev to Saddam Hussein, in which the Soviet leader demanded a withdrawal from Kuwait and the release of all foreigners, and added: "We have deferred a vote at the UN Security Council as long as we could. We ask you to give us your response by Friday evening [August 24] at the latest."

Shevardnadze called his American opposite number as soon as he had received the Iraqi reply.

"What do they say?" asked Baker.

Shevardnadze seemed appalled by what he had read. "It doesn't even deserve comment. In any case, it doesn't satisfy us at all. You can go to the United Nations. We'll support you."

A few minutes later the head of the American delegation at the UN, Thomas Pickering, received orders from Baker to keep the fifteen members of the Security Council in session for as long as it took to get the resolution passed. On Saturday, August 25, at 4:00 A.M., Resolution 665, authorizing the use of force in order to implement the embargo, was passed by thirteen votes to zero. Cuba and Yemen abstained.

On August 27 the Reverend Jesse Jackson set off from Kennedy Airport on a Jordanian Airlines plane. The former presidential candidate was setting a fashion that would be all the rage in the months to come: a trip to Baghdad, a meeting with Saddam Hussein to hear his grievances, then a return home together with an armful of hostages. The first to open the breach had been Austrian Chancellor Kurt Waldheim, glad of the chance to lift the international quarantine imposed on him because of his controversial past.

Jesse Jackson's trip carried more weight because he was a public figure in the United States, and the present crisis was seen as essentially a match between Bush and Saddam Hussein. Jackson was flying to Baghdad with a television crew, and his objective was to get an interview with Saddam Hussein. The way his trip developed revealed the use that Baghdad was planning to make of such visits.

There were 3 million foreigners in Iraq and Kuwait. The largest contingents were the Egyptians (1.5 million in Iraq and 150,000 in Kuwait), the Palestinians (300,000 in Iraq and 170,000 in Kuwait), the Indians, and the Filipinos. But these Third World workers were an infinitely less effective bargaining counter than the Americans (2,500 in Kuwait and 500 in Iraq), the British (4,000 in Kuwait and 500 in Iraq), and the other European nationals.

Soon after their arrival Jackson and his delegation had a long meeting with Tariq Aziz. For three and a half hours the Foreign Minister carefully explained his country's position and the historical background to the crisis, even going so far as to say, "Several times during the negotiations President Saddam Hussein showed that he was more patient and more moderate than me. . . . At the end of the Jeddah summit [on July 31, the eve of the invasion] we were driven to despair by Kuwait's intransigence. We couldn't even pay for our food imports. There was a real campaign to starve us. Even King Fahd of Saudi Arabia didn't seem worried to hear that we were hungry. We came to the conclusion that there was a plot to destroy Iraq, a plot that Kuwait would not have mounted without the support of a superpower. It was clear to us that the aim of the plot was to provoke Iraq's economic collapse, followed by a political collapse and a change of regime."

When Tariq Aziz had finished, one of the journalists with Jackson asked, "How can Iraq hope for sympathy when Americans still remember the sight of Kurdish civilians gassed in 1988 and the hanging of a British journalist earlier this year?"

Taken by surprise, Tariq Aziz was silent for a moment, then answered in a low voice, "I admit it's a problem."

That evening Jesse Jackson had a private meeting with Saddam Hussein. In the course of the conversation they touched on the martyrdom of Jesus Christ. The Iraqi leader considered that he, like Christ, was a victim of prejudice and false accusations. He admitted that he had given orders to detain foreigners, but that, to him, was "a guarantee of peace." "The current blockade on food and medicine," he said, "is a more ruthless act than the taking of hostages." It was obvious that Saddam Hussein was extremely bitter toward the United States. He felt insulted by the lack of an American response to his "many overtures." "After my talk with your Ambassador on July 25," he said in a humble voice, "the American authorities didn't even ask for an official transcript of the meeting. Your country treats me with the condescension of a colonial power toward a colony."

The following day, after a brief stopover in Kuwait City, Jackson got his interview. For reasons of security, Saddam Hussein's entourage demanded that the filming be handled by cameramen and equipment from Iraqi television. At the end of the interview Jackson asked the President if, in a goodwill gesture that "would serve the interests of peace," he would be ready to free the hostages immediately.

Saddam Hussein replied, irritated: "I've explained my position on that subject clearly in many interviews with many journalists. There's nothing else to add." He stood up, and for a moment his attitude and expression changed. There was no more irritation but a satisfied smile and a long handshake with Jackson for the benefit of the cameras. He solemnly announced for all to hear: "This has been a good evening and a profound human exchange. In honor of the Americans who are watching us on television, you can take with you those women and children I authorize to leave, as well as four men who are apparently ill. You can fly to the United States on an Iraqi plane."

While Jackson was getting ready to leave Baghdad, the Director General of the Israeli Defense Ministry, David Ivri, was landing in Tel Aviv. He had been hastily dispatched to Washington for secret talks with top Pentagon officials. The Israeli government was worried about American plans to sell arms to Saudi Arabia, in particular twenty-four F-15Cs, 150 tanks and 200 Stinger anti-aircraft missiles. The Israelis estimated that the sale was worth nearly $2.5 billion. David Ivri had taken with him a request: Israel wanted permission to acquire more military materiel immediately, especially F-16s and Apache and Tow missiles, as well as to receive, in a single installment at the beginning of the fiscal year, the $1.8 billion in military aid agreed to by the United States. Ivri returned with a promise that the United States would sell Israel $1 billion worth of sophisticated weapons.

The same day the Israeli government received a message from

Gorbachev, passed on by French Foreign Minister Roland Dumas, who had just met him. Moscow was worried by reports from Baghdad that suggested the possibility of an Iraqi attack on Israel.

For Gorbachev the Gulf crisis was not only a wonderful opportunity to demonstrate to the world his moderation and sense of responsibility by working in close collaboration with Washington; it was also a headache and perhaps a trap. He had to resist onslaughts from certain influential power bases, notably within the army, in sections of the KGB and at the Foreign Ministry, which still had close ties with Baghdad. They were all "worried by his collusion with the American strategy." On August 31 he restated his belief that the action of the United States was "in accordance with the United Nations Charter." By way of retort, it was pointed out to him that Washington was setting up a collective security structure in the Gulf that would lead to a permanent American military presence in the region. That could put him in a very awkward position.

In addition he was angry that the Kremlin had known nothing of Iraq's plans. On the day of the invasion, he had summoned the Defense Minister, Marshal Dmitri Yazov, a staunch conservative, to his office. The conversation had not been a friendly one.

Inquiries revealed that the GRU, the military intelligence service, had been informed of Iraq's preparation for the invasion two weeks before it took place. The GRU had many contacts in Iraq, including military experts and officials close to Saddam. The heads of the GRU justified their silence by saying that the information they had obtained had seemed "exaggerated." It was a plausible explanation, but their silence might also have been voluntary, with the aim of embarrassing Gorbachev. Moreover, the Iraqis held a bargaining counter: the

Soviet military advisers who were still in Iraq and whose exact number was a secret. Baghdad had made it clear to Moscow that their return would be hampered if the Soviets passed on "military secrets" to the United States.

The most skeptical Western analysts suspected Gorbachev of being two-faced. On the one hand, he was playing the diplomatic card and sharing the indignation of the international community. On the other, he was continuing, in secret, to provide military assistance to the Baghdad regime, an ally of twenty years' standing. Whatever the truth, it was obvious that these suspicions weakened Gorbachev's credibility.

On the evening of September 5 he appeared on the TV news program *Vremia* and gave a complete account of his day and the visitors he had received. He did not mention his meeting with Tariq Aziz, who had made a brief trip to Moscow and had been received "at his own request" by the Soviet President. Coming out of an interview that was described as "frank"—in official Soviet jargon that meant "difficult"—Aziz declared with a smile: "Without hesitation, I can still call the USSR a friend." It was a phrase whose apparent candor was perhaps designed to discomfit Gorbachev three days before his summit meeting with George Bush in Helsinki. The day before Eduard Shevardnadze, speaking in Vladivostok, had stated: "The international community cannot tolerate predator states and pirate regimes."

The USSR was not the only country suspected of playing a double game. During the weeks to come various authoritative sources would wonder about the true position of the French. Some would even describe it as "dubious" or "equivocal." Had France negotiated with Iraq for the release of her hostages? In Tunis and in Amman French envoys known for their privileged links with Arab leaders and with the secret services of the Middle East had probably had direct contact with Iraqi officials. The names most often cited were Claude Cheysson and Philippe Rondot. The latter was an Arab specialist in the French secret service whose father, many years before, had helped set up its equivalent in Syria. What price had been paid? Certainly more than the symbolic thirty-mile withdrawal of the 5,000 French soldiers stationed in Saudi Arabia or the abandonment of the French Embassy in Kuwait on the pretext of lack of water.

Another mystery, and a more serious one, was whether there were still French citizens in Iraq. Civilian and perhaps also military technicians, established in Baghdad before the invasion of Kuwait to maintain French military equipment, were said to be active after the hostages had been freed, in violation of UN resolutions.

On September 8, a few hours before Bush and Gorbachev arrived in Helsinki, Saddam Hussein issued a warning on Iraqi television that there should be no foreign interference in the Arab world and that the USSR should do all it could to retain its status as a superpower. It was a hostile and treacherous remark, which implied that, by subscribing to the American position, Moscow was gradually losing its influence and slipping into a subordinate role.

On September 9 Bush and Gorbachev reached an agreement. Gorbachev, having managed to convince the American President that he was not supporting Iraq militarily, was given the green light to maintain diplomatic links with Baghdad. One of his closest colleagues, Yevgeni Primakov, would be given the task of pursuing the matter. In return Gorbachev authorized Bush to continue with his preparations for war. A joint statement reaffirmed the desire to reach a peaceful settlement of the crisis. Nevertheless, "If all the steps now being pursued fail, we are ready to consider other measures in accordance with the Charter of the United Nations."

The mystery factor was still the determination of Saddam Hussein. Some indication of the truth may be gleaned from the confidences he shared with Yasser Arafat and Abu Iyad at a meeting at the end of August.

The PLO chiefs found him "completely relaxed." "Now that the Gulf crisis has taken on such dimensions," he said calmly, "can I reduce it to a mere demand for two islands and a few oil wells, especially as I've withdrawn from the Shatt al-Arab? It's not enough. If I tell the Iraqi people that I'm withdrawing because I've settled a problem as important as the Palestinian question, they'll understand. But if I go only in order to keep a few islands and a few oilfields, the people will never accept it. It would be worse than losing the war. I've never said that I'm ready to withdraw. Why? Because I believe the Iraqi soldiers will lose their morale if they feel that I believe in withdrawal." Saddam added: "If I make a peace proposal, then I'm the one who'll have to make concessions. If the others propose one, then I can obtain concessions."

The three men discussed the possibility of war. Saddam contemplated it with equanimity. "I'm perfectly well aware," he said, "of American technological superiority, especially in the air, but I think they'll be able to neutralize only part of the Iraqi forces. The decisive battle will take place on the ground."

He described in detail the nature and scale of the various offensives that might be launched against him. He seemed to have considered everything: the possible losses, the means of retaliation. "As I listened to him," Arafat would later say, "I was astounded by how calm he was."

The head of the PLO told him that there was reliable information suggesting that a plot was being hatched to eliminate him. Saddam Hussein burst out laughing and replied, "Are you trying to frighten me into surrendering? What a joke!"

Gorbachev's special envoy, Yevgeni Primakov, had several meetings with Saddam Hussein. At one such meeting in October Primakov, astonished and exasperated by the Iraqi leader's intransigence, dropped the diplomatic language he had been using and said, "Mr. President, if you persist, the Americans will wage war on you, and we won't intervene to prevent it."

"I know," replied Saddam Hussein, almost indifferently.

"But you'll lose," retorted Primakov.

Saddam Hussein looked at him for a long time and then replied calmly, "Perhaps."

9

Countdown to War

By mid-October it was clear that the crisis would continue for some time. It was also clear that solution of the crisis was getting more and more complicated. Dramatic things had happened in the Middle East.

Now the front pages of newspapers and radio and television were focusing on new problems: the death of twenty-one Palestinians on Temple Mount in Jerusalem on October 8 and the ousting from power of the Christian military leader in Beirut, General Aoun, by Syrian forces on October 13.

On August 12, ten days after the invasion of Kuwait, Saddam Hussein had declared the matter could be settled only in the context of other Middle East conflicts—the Israeli occupation of the West Bank and Gaza and the Golan Heights, the Syrian occupation of Lebanon, and the Israeli occupation of southern Lebanon. The U.S. and Israeli governments had reacted by calling Saddam Hussein's proposal "cheap propaganda."

But as the crisis moved forward, some Western powers made statements that seemed to link these Middle East problems. President François Mitterrand of France, in a speech to the

United Nations on September 24, said that if Saddam Hussein declared he was going to withdraw from Kuwait, all negotiations would be open. The British Foreign Secretary, Douglas Hurd, said settlement of the Palestinian problem would be a top priority once the Gulf crisis was resolved. And even President Bush, while making no direct link, said that after Saddam Hussein had withdrawn from Kuwait, other Middle East problems needed to be solved.

The bloody outbreak of October 8 in Jerusalem was a gift for Saddam Hussein. It focused the attention of the world on the Palestinian problem and put Israel in an extremely sensitive position. The Israelis immediately adopted the position that the outbreak that day had been masterminded by the PLO to embarrass Israel. Some Israeli spokesman even went as far as saying that Iraq was probably behind the PLO effort. Palestinian leaders had another view. They accused the Israelis of a bloody response to what they perceived as an effort to prevent a group of Israeli extremists, the "Temple Mount Faithful," from marching on a mosque on Temple Mount that they had declared should be torn down and replaced by a new synagogue. It was clear that the Iraqi police prevented the extremists from getting near the mosque. It was clear that the Palestinians started hurling rocks at thousands of Jews praying in front of the Holy Wall. But it was also clear Israeli forces opened fire on the Palestinians after the Jews had escaped from the rocks and were no longer in danger.

Some Israeli groups attacked their own government for the way in which the demonstration was handled. An independent Israeli group, B'Tselem, which monitors Israeli action in the Occupied Territories, accused Israeli forces of firing indiscriminately at Palestinian rioters, bystanders, and medical workers. "The firing continued even while the crowd was dispersing in every direction and many were fleeing, as well as at the stage in which ambulances and medical teams arrived on the scene," the group said in a damning thirty-four page report.

The event created an enormous problem for the United States government, which for many years has had warm relations with Israel. Trapped in a United Nations Security Council debate for five days, it tried to produce as soft a resolution against the Israelis as possible. But, having gathered together a number of Arab nations to support it in the Gulf crisis, it was no longer in a position to veto a resolution. In the days that followed the uprising in Jerusalem, one could see, across the Arab world, that attacks against the PLO for supporting Saddam Hussein were temporarily shifting around. The target became Israel once again. This was particularly true in Egypt, where President Hosni Mubarak had become a strong supporter of the United States position on Saddam Hussein.

When the UN resolution was finally adopted, it not only critized Israel for the way it had handled the Palestinians but called on a United Nations delegation to go to Israel and investigate the event. The conservative government of Itzak Shamir reacted with rage. It attacked the United States for its position and completely rejected a UN investigative team, saying that UN representatives could come to the country only as tourists. U.S. Secretary of State James Baker compared the Israeli reaction to the UN resolution with the way Saddam Hussein had reacted to the UN. This only increased the tension between the United States and Israel, something the United States government had fervently hoped would not happen. From the beginning of the crisis the U.S. had counseled Israel to keep a low profile. It did not want to see the Gulf crisis perceived as an American–Zionist plot. Saddam Hussein had understood that, which is why on several occasions he had announced publicly that if Iraq were attacked by the U.S. and other military forces in Saudi Arabia, he would immediately launch a missile attack on Israel. By doing so, he hoped he would involve Israel in the war and immediately erode the support of Arab nations for the attack against his own country.

The Israeli government set up an inquiry into the Jerusalem bloodbath headed by former Mossad director Zvi Zamir. The first testimony was heard behind closed doors on Sunday, October 14. Twelve days later the Zamir report virtually declared the Israeli troops innocent of the killing of the twenty-one Palestinians.

It was probably anger with the United States that stimulated the Israelis to make another decision that was certain to hurt their relations with the United States further. The Housing Minister, Ariel Sharon, announced plans for the construction of buildings in East Jerusalem to house Jews emigrating from the Soviet Union. The Americans had given Israel a $400 million loan guarantee for housing in Israel but with the condition that none of this money be used to build homes in occupied territories. Sharon held that East Jerusalem was not an occupied territory but a part of the Israeli capital of Jerusalem, something that virtually every foreign power in the world has refused to accept.

Syria's decision to use its military forces in Lebanon to oust General Aoun was also linked to the Gulf crisis. Syria, which for years had been condemned by the United States as a terrorist power, had become an ally of the United States in the Gulf crisis. President Hafez Al Assad had always hated Saddam Hussein and was only too happy to join a worldwide group with the intention of forcing his retreat from Kuwait and perhaps even ousting him from power. U.S. Secretary of State James Baker had gone to Damascus for a long meeting with President Assad, which had prompted some criticism in the United States.

Families of the victims of the Pan Am 103 flight, which had exploded over Lockerbie, Scotland, in November 1988 were particulary enraged. They could not believe that a top U.S official would visit a country that had played a role in that terrorist attack.

But now President Assad was in a more comfortable position *vis-à-vis* the United States. He had deployed troops in Saudi Arabia and the United Arab Emirates, and he had vigorously supported the position of the United States and the United Nations against Iraq. A top Syrian source has revealed that when Assad gathered his troops around the Christian section of Beirut dominated by General Aoun, he got the green light from the White House to go in and oust the General from power.

When General Aoun saw his area surrounded by the Syrians he appealed to the Israelis for help. This is confirmed by Uri Lubrani, the Israeli coordinator of operations in Lebanon. He added that the Syrian–U.S. alliance in the Gulf crisis made it eaasier for Syria to use force to oust General Aoun. "I have no doubt that the Syrians felt much freer to use force inside Lebanon when they were in an alliance with the United States," Lubrani said.

After a short but bloody battle the General fled from the presidential palace to the French Embassy in Beirut. He is still there. The new Lebanese government of President Elias Hrawl has repeatedly refused the French government's request that he be allowed to leave Lebanon and move to France. It insists he be tried for corruption.

The Syrian intervention in East Beirut attracted no public criticism from the United States or any other major power. Instead it was portrayed as a generous effort to put Lebanon back together. It is certainly important that the desecrated country be reestablished, but it would be difficult to interpret Syrian occupation of Lebanon for many years any differently from Iraqi occupation of Kuwait, even if the Syrians insist that they entered Lebanon to try to bring about peace.

If Syria had successfully gotten the green light to move into Lebanon as a result of its joining the coalition, the action had also had some other positive results. The reason why it had joined the coalition was not just that it had long had bad relations with Iraq. First, Syria felt isolated from a number of important Arab powers, particularly Egypt and Saudi Arabia. The Arab Cooperation Council, formed in 1989, and the Gulf Cooperation Council were both organizations in which Syria had no place. In joining the coalition against Iraq Syria had broken down barriers and was now associated with important Arab countries. The Syrians also understood what was going on in the Eastern bloc nations and the Soviet Union, which had been supporters of the Assad regime. Those countries were now in deep economic trouble and the Syrians realized that their economic and military help to Syria was going to disintegrate. Therefore it was important to find another powerful ally—the United States. The Syrian government understood that by joining the coalition it would work toward more normal relations with the U.S.

Despite these improvements, there was growing frustration in Syria on other issues. The first was that the United States had allocated $700 million to Israel to help improve its anti-missile system. The Syrians strongly condemned this decision, saying it was a way for the United States to link the Gulf crisis with the Arab–Israeli conflict. Syria was also frustrated with all the financial help that countries like Egypt were getting from the West. The United States had canceled a $7 billion Egyptian debt, and the Gulf states had handed Egypt about $5 billion in cash. Syria still faced economic sanctions on the part of the United States and Great Britain and was not getting the financial help that would solve some of the basic problems of the Syrian economy.

The Syrians were also angry about diplomatic relations. They had seen Britain restore diplomatic relations with Iran, but Britain had refused to restore diplomatic relations with Syria. Those relations had been broken at the time of the Hendawi affair in 1986, when a bomb was found being placed on an El Al plane at Heathrow Airport in London. The British blamed the Syrians for this terrorist operation.

Prime Minister Margaret Thatcher had refused to shift from that position despite the new Syrian policy of defending the anti-Iraq coalition. The diplomatic problem would finally be solved when Mrs. Thatcher was ousted from office in November. Twenty-four hours later Britain reestablished diplomatic relations with Syria.

Finally, the Syrians had another concern. While they hated Iraq, they still considered that country an important ally if they got involved in a war with Israel. Thus the Syrians made it clear that their troops in Saudi Arabia were there to defend that country, not to attack Iraq, that they wanted not a war against Iraq but a peaceful solution. It wanted to see the Kuwaiti problem solved but Iraq still in a position of military power. The Syrian position would change dramatically when the war finally started. Syria would quietly accept the destruction of Iraq and support the idea of overthrowing Saddam Hussein.

There were other important events that were affecting the Gulf crisis.

On November 18, three and a half months after the invasion of Kuwait, thirty-four heads of state and prime ministers from

Western and Eastern Europe, the United States, and Canada were gathering for the first CSCE summit since the end of the Cold War. An urgent message came through: Saddam Hussein had just announced in Baghdad that all foreign hostages would be freed, starting on Christmas Day. The decision was not surprising. Since the beginning of the crisis, Saddam Hussein had intelligently manipulated the hostage issue in an effort to decrease worldwide support for any military attack on his country. This latest move would surely be spurned by the United States as just more Iraqi propaganda. Sure enough, the next morning, after having breakfast with Prime Minister Margaret Thatcher, President Bush denounced Iraq's decision to release foreign hostages in stages and said that if Saddam Hussein wanted a peaceful solution, he should do in Kuwait what he had done in Iran, "turn tail 180 degrees. There won't have to be a shot fired in anger if he does what he is supposed to do, which is to comply fully with our conditions to the United Nations resolutions."

As the CSCE meeting gathered it was clear that the Gulf crisis was becoming more and more complicated. For months we had heard about the various options for the solution of the crisis—peaceful negotiations, unilateral retreat from Kuwait by Iraqi forces, an Arab solution, and war. After initially deploying almost 200,000 troops in the Middle East, President George Bush, early in November, had announced the reinforcement of the military presence in Saudi Arabia with at least 200,000 more troops. For those following the Gulf crisis, it was a clear message. The United States had dramatically changed its position: now it had shifted to offensive power, and the possibility of war was becoming more certain. Some experts said the deployment of the troops meant that war would break out between mid- to late January and early February. Others believed that it was perhaps a ploy to cover up an early attack on Kuwait.

President Bush and Secretary of State James Baker had come to Paris not only to attend the conference but also to convince France and the Soviet Union that a new UN resolution was needed that would back military action against Iraq. After Baker met with the French Foreign Minister, Roland Dumas, his aides passed the word that France had agreed to support such a resolution. The same kind of message was received after President Bush had dinner with French President François Mitterrand. But then word came from the Elysée that no accord had been made. While France agreed with the idea "in principle," it would not back the resolution until it had been debated at the United Nations. President Mitterrand finally cleared up the matter at a press conference after the CSCE summit ended. He said a new UN resolution would be adopted within three weeks and that it would probably include backing for the use of force.

The same thing happened with the Soviets. Baker had three meetings with Soviet Foreign Minister Eduard Shevardnadze, and Bush met Soviet President Mikhail Gorbachev. At first the word was that the Soviets were not enthusiastic about a UN resolution backing force. Soviet spokesman kept saying their country's position was "patience." But before leaving Paris Gorbachev appeared on French television and lashed out against Iraq and Saddam Hussein. "The situation is very dangerous," Gorbachev said. "We have to act. We have to be resolute and firm. There is need for the UN Security Council to discuss the situation without delay and make a decision."

Those who hoped there might be an Arab solution were now disillusioned. In early November King Hassan of Morocco had called for an Arab summit to solve the Gulf problem. While Iraq immediately supported the idea, key Arab states such as Egypt, Syria, and Saudi Arabia immediately rejected it.

Those who hoped for a diplomatic solution were also disillusioned. Yevgeni Primakov, the Soviet mediator who had been traveling nonstop through the Middle East states, including Iraq, in an effort to find a peaceful solution, talked about proposing concessions to Iraq. But this was something the United States would not, and could not, accept. In fact, President Bush had put himself in a position that was hard to change and virtually impossible to negotiate. Bush said no talks could be conducted with Iraq until Saddam Hussein had withdrawn from Kuwait, the Kuwaiti royal family was restored to power, and all foreign hostages were released. Many interviews with Saddam Hussein indicated he would not accept that position. When I was in Baghdad at the beginning of September, I was told by the Foreign Ministry that Saddam Hussein wanted a televised debate with President Bush. The subject had been passed to the White House and the response had been a loud "no." In an interview with ABC anchor man Peter Jennings in Baghdad on November 15 Saddam Hussein had stressed he was ready to negotiate with the United States and Saudi Arabia but with "no pre-conditions." That meant that he would not pull out of Kuwait until he had arrived at a negotiated solution. Despite all the talk about the need for a diplomatic solution, it was all but impossible.

With no unconditional withdrawal by Saddam Hussein, no Arab solution, no diplomatic solution, there was clearly only one option: war.

On November 29 the United Nations adopted Resolution 678, which clearly supported that option. The vote was 12–2, with Cuba and Yemen opposing the resolution and China abstaining. The key paragraph in the resolution authorized "member states cooperating with the government of Kuwait" to use "all necessary means" to implement UN resolution 660, which called for the complete withdrawal of Iraq from Kuwait. The date set for the withdrawal under Resolution 678 was "on or before" January 15, 1991. The resolution also called for the restoration of "international peace and security in the area," key words that Western powers would later quote to buttress their position, that of going beyond liberating Kuwait to invade Iraq.

It was now countdown time to war.

10

The Days Tick By

When UN Resolution 678 was adopted on November 29, 1990, it became clear that war had become a serious option in the Gulf crisis. If the United States and the other coalition powers had felt a negotiated solution was possible—some experts believed that they did not want a negotiated solution—this resolution would not have been adopted. Many political leaders around the world thought that setting a precise date for Saddam Hussein's withdrawal from Kuwait was a sign that the United States had given up on its original plan of waiting until the sanctions approved by the United Nations really began to have an effect on the Iraqi people. It was clear that sanctions would have to last much longer than officials had predicted at the beginning.

But the United States faced a number of difficult problems. In waiting for the sanctions to be effective, it would have to leave troops on Saudi soil for a long time. This would have an effect on the U.S. economy, since the deployment of the troops was costing the U.S. government a great deal of money, despite the fact that it was getting important monetary support from countries like Saudi Arabia, Kuwait, Germany, and Japan.

There was also a religious problem. Ramadan, one of the most important Moslem religious periods, would start in mid-March. This would seriously affect the Arab partners in the coalition, particularly Saudi Arabia, Egypt, and Syria. Even later, in May, came Haj, when each year millions of Moslems travel to the holy sites of Mecca and Medina in Saudi Arabia, the centers of the Moslem world. There would be a revolt against the presence of non-Arab military on Saudi soil while Haj was taking place.

Finally, there was the problem of weather. Once past March, the Kuwait–Saudi Arabia area would become unbearably hot. The heat could have a deleterious effect on U.S. and other military equipment, as well as on troops not used to desert life. So experts in the U.S. government had decided that a solution was needed before mid-March.

The day after the UN adopted Resolution 678, November 30, President Bush intelligently put forward a peace plan to convince the world that war was not inevitable. He proposed a meeting with Iraqi foreign minister Tariq Aziz and offered to send Secretary of State James Baker to Baghdad to see Saddam Hussein. The world welcomed the proposal as a clear sign that President Bush was still seeking a diplomatic solution to the crisis.

I arrived in Tunis late in the afternoon of that day and the next morning met with Abu Iyad, the number-two leader of the PLO. I had known Abu Iyad for many years. A Palestinian who had lived part of his life in Kuwait (his family, including his wife, still lived there), he was in the early 1970s the mastermind of the PLO's worldwide terrorist activities. He had become the head of Black September and organized the attack against the Israeli athletes at the Munich Olympic Games of 1972. But in the early 1980s he had become convinced that terrorism was not the way to solve the Palestinian problem and had moved toward a more moderate profile. He played a key role in pushing the PLO to change its position, to abandon terrorism, to recognize the existence of Israel, and to open dialogue with the United States. He was a valuable right-hand man to the PLO leader, Yasser Arafat, and he influenced Arafat's move toward moderation.

Abu Iyad started to brief me about what happened in the PLO headquarters when they learned about the Bush proposal. Arafat had immediately convened a meeting of the top PLO leaders present in Tunis. After several hours of discussion they had written a secret memorandum to Saddam Hussein, which had been conveyed to the Iraqi leader through the Iraqi Embassy in Tunis. It contained three critical points. First: accept the Bush proposal. It is probably the last chance to arrive at a peaceful solution of this crisis. Second: get rid of all the foreign hostages before there is a meeting between Tariq Aziz and President Bush. Getting rid of the hostages will make the possibility of arriving at a diplomatic solution easier. Third: prepare your pullout from Kuwait, but don't forget the secret deal you have with King Fahd of Saudi Arabia to keep the frontier areas that have been the subject of a long-standing controversy between Iraq and Kuwait.

Abu Iyad told me that Arafat was on his way to Amman for a meeting with King Hussein of Jordan before going on to Baghdad to see Saddam Hussein. He said he would leave the next day for Yemen to try to get the leadership there to support the PLO plan that had been sent to Saddam Hussein.

I asked Abu Iyad if he was going to meet the PLO leader in the Iraqi capital, as he always had before. His answer was surprising. "I'm never going to Baghdad again. I'm never going to meet with Saddam Hussein again." I asked him why he had taken this decision, and he revealed a fascinating piece of information.

On November 16 he had been in Baghdad with Arafat at a meeting with Saddam Hussein. During that meeting he had entered into a tough argument with the Iraqi leader. "You are not helping the Palestinian movement as you claim. You are destroying it. You are destroying thousands of Palestinians in Kuwait. You are destroying my family. They have all lost their jobs and are now starving to death." Abu Iyad said he had also seriously criticized Saddam Hussein's support of the Abu Nidal terrorist movement. Abu Nidal, one of the most dangerous terrorists in the world, had quit the PLO in the early 1970s and, soon after setting up his own organization, the Fatah Revolutionary Council, had pronounced a death sentence on Abu Iyad. Iyad was well aware that, in the years since Abu Nidal had created his terrorist groups, he had been involved in several efforts to assassinate the leaders of the PLO, including himself. Saddam Hussein was outraged by Abu Iyad's statements and threw him out of the office. Arafat had also been upset by his deputy's statements but had managed to get him out of the country safely.

That was the last time I saw Abu Iyad alive. On the night of January 15, two days before the Gulf war broke out, he was assassinated in Tunis along with the chief of PLO security, Hayel Abed-Hamid, also known as Abu Hol. It had been a tragic security mistake on the part of the PLO to allow the killer, Hamza Abu Zid, pretending to be a defector from the Abu Nidal movement, to become Abu Hol's bodyguard. The investigation into the assassination is still continuing, but there is general evidence that it was an operation organized by the

Abu Nidal movement. What is not clear is whether the assassination was an independent decision taken by the Abu Nidal movement or an order issued by someone else.

On December 4, Arafat, King Hussein, and the Vice-President of Yemen, Ali Salem Al Beldh, met for four hours with Saddam Hussein in Baghdad, pushing for the implementation of their recommendations. Forty-eight hours later, on December 6, Saddam announced the immediate release of all foreign hostages. Since he had earlier said that foreign hostages would be allowed to leave around Christmastime, there was some early skepticism about his announcement, but in the days that followed it became clear that, in fact, all the hostages were being freed and that one of the elements of the Gulf crisis was being solved.

On the diplomatic front, however, despite much activity, nothing seemed to be moving forward. First and most important, the United States and Iraq could not seem to reach agreement on when Tariq Aziz would go to Washington and James Baker to Baghdad. From the U.S. point of view, this was all Iraq's fault. The Americans said they had proposed fifteen dates and that Saddam Hussein had accepted none of them. Saddam Hussein had called for a meeting with James Baker on January 12, which the U.S. felt was too close to the January 15 deadline for Iraq's withdrawal from Kuwait. On the Iraqi side this was seen as just another indication that the U.S. did not want to have any real talks with them. They said that one may not impose dates on an Arab country; dates must be negotiated. And they said the U.S. was unwilling to negotiate, even on the dates.

A top Iraqi source told me that all that was needed to set up conversations involving Tariq Aziz, George Bush, James

Baker, and Saddam Hussein was for Bush to pick up the phone and call Saddam Hussein to discuss it with him. This was part of Saddam Hussein's mentality. From the beginning of the crisis he had felt that the only way to arrive at a negotiated solution to the crisis was to have direct talks with two people—King Fahd of Saudi Arabia and President Bush of the United States.

In any case, a solution to President Bush's proposal was never reached, and finally only one direct U.S.–Iraqi contact would take place—a meeting between James Baker and Tariq Aziz on January 9. But before that meeting there was to be much other diplomatic effort.

On December 12 the Algerian President, Chadli Bendjedid, launched a peace offensive at a meeting with Saddam Hussein in Baghdad. For those who understood Middle East negotiations the entry of Algeria into the process was very important. For years Algeria had played a very positive role in dealing with crises in the area. Perhaps the most important example was its work in late 1980 and early 1981 to bring to an end the debacle involving United States hostages in Iran. It was due largely to Algeria that the hostages were released at the very time that Ronald Reagan was being inaugurated as President of the United States on January 20, 1981.

President Bendjedid soon ran into a wall in his effort to negotiate. The Saudi Arabian government refused to receive him, saying negotiations were not possible before Saddam Hussein withdrew from Kuwait. And the United States government told Algeria that President Bendjedid should not come to Washington. It would be sufficient, they said, for him to have a telephone conversation with President Bush.

On December 18 things became more complicated. The United States and Iraq had not yet come to an agreement on dates for meetings between Tariq Aziz and President Bush. Tariq Aziz had sent word to the European Community that he was ready to meet with the Foreign Ministers. But that day, in Brussels, the EEC Foreign Ministers rejected a meeting with the Iraqi foreign minister, indicating that they did not want to give the impression that a split was developing in the anti-Iraq alliance.

That decision would have important consequences. In the days before the January 15 deadline, when a flurry of diplomatic activity was taking place around the world, the EEC Foreign Ministers changed their minds and decided it was important for them to meet Tariq Aziz. But Aziz refused several times, still angered by the December 18 decision in Brussels.

Two days later, on December 20, a dramatic event occurred in the Soviet Union, demonstrating that the crisis the world was still facing was not located in the Middle East alone. The Minister of Foreign Affairs, Eduard Shevardnadze, resigned, accusing Soviet leader Mikhail Gorbachev of moving toward dictatorship. This was a particular loss for Secretary of State James Baker, who had developed with Shevardnadze the best relationship ever achieved between a U.S. Secretary of State and a Soviet Foreign Minister. Shevardnadze's resignation also indicated that some hard-line communist leaders in the Soviet Union were beginning to question Gorbachev's decision to join the United States in the anti-Iraq alliance, particularly since Iraq had long been an ally of the Soviet Union and one of its biggest customers in arms deals.

The days ticked by, one by one, into 1991. The first of January was a holiday, but January 2 saw a wave of diplomatic efforts start up again. Luxembourg's Foreign Minister, Jacques Poos, who had become President of the EEC the day before, called a Foreign Ministers' meeting for Friday, January 4. Poos said he expected the Foreign Ministers to send him to Baghdad for talks with Tariq Aziz.

Jordan's King Hussein was heading for Europe for talks in London, Rome, Paris, Bonn, and Luxembourg. King Hussein had not ceased trying to find a diplomatic solution to the crisis since his extraordinary effort in the first forty-eight hours of the crisis. The King said Algeria and Yugoslavia, representing the non-aligned movement, were also still involved in the peace process.

While all these efforts was being made, President Bush was telling the American people, in an interview with the British journalist David Frost, that reversing Iraq's takeover of Kuwait was the greatest moral challenge since the Second World War. When asked what would happen if fighting broke out in the Gulf, he said he hoped it would be over in a few days.

The next day, January 3, frustrated by the failure to agree on dates for U.S.–Iraq meetings, President Bush stepped forward again to offer Iraq a final chance for talks with the U.S. before the January 15 deadline. He suggested a meeting between Secretary of State Baker and Tariq Aziz on January 7, 8 or 9. But he said that such a meeting would not include negotiations, compromise, face-saving, or rewards for aggression. It was certainly not a statement that suggested that such a meeting would resolve the crisis.

Two days later the Iraqis accepted. They said Aziz would meet Baker in Geneva on January 9. Only six days away from the January 15 deadline, it was going to be a crucial event.

11

"Put Your Car in the Garage Tonight"

U.S. Secretary of State James Baker and Iraqi Foreign Minister Tariq Aziz arrived in Geneva in the evening. Their meeting was to start the next morning at the Inter-Continental Hotel. The world media had packed into Geneva, understanding this was the first—and probably the last—direct high-level contact between the United States and Iraq since the invasion of Kuwait on August 2, 1990. Most experts predicted that the meeting would not be a negotiation but rather an exchange of hard positions between the two countries.

When the meeting began the next morning, each leader flanked by delegations, the press was allowed in to the room to see and film the opening of the encounter. Although Baker and Aziz leaned across the table and shook hands, there were no smiles. The press emerged from the photo opportunity convinced they were right: the meeting would be a failure.

But then a surprise occurred. The meeting lasted much longer than expected. As it went on, hour by hour, it began to seem as though Baker and Aziz were really trying to achieve a solution. There were several breaks in the talks and an hour off for lunch, but the meeting kept going on, and a Middle East expert announced on British television that he had learned, through inside sources, that a deal had been cut that would lead to a peaceful end to the crisis.

The press covering the meeting was becoming more and more optimistic. Journalists were convinced that at each break Baker was conferring with President Bush and that, even though Tariq Aziz was not calling Baghdad, he had come to Geneva with a package given to him by Saddam Hussein. After more than six hours of discussion the meeting came to an end. The press waited for Secretary of State Baker to emerge and tell them what had happened in a press conference.

Baker's opening statement shattered any hope that a peaceful solution was possible:

Ladies and gentlemen. I have just given President Bush a full report of our meeting today. I told him that Minister Aziz and I had completed a serious and extended diplomatic conversation in an effort to find a political solution to the crisis in the Gulf. I have met with Minister Aziz today not to negotiate, as we made clear we would not do—that is, negotiate backwards from United Nations Security Council resolutions—but I met with him today to communicate, and communicate means listening as well as talking. And we did that, both of us. The message that I conveyed from President Bush and our coalition partners was that Iraq must either comply with the will of the international community and withdraw peacefully from Kuwait or be expelled by force.

Regrettably, ladies and gentlemen, I heard nothing today that—in over six hours I heard nothing that suggested to me any Iraqi flexibility whatsoever on complying with the UN Security Council resolutions.

The message was clear. The meeting had failed.

Baker stated that Tariq Aziz had refused to accept a letter Baker had handed him to give to Saddam Hussein. Aziz read the letter, then handed it back to Baker. Aziz would later say at a press conference that "the language in this letter is not compatible with the language that should be used in correspondence between heads of state."

But now, having had contact with top sources, it is clear to me why the meeting did not work. Tariq Aziz had not come to Geneva with any proposals. He had come with only one objective—to persuade the United States to withdraw the January 15 deadline adopted by the United Nations. Saddam Hussein was not a man who adopted deadlines. He considered them intimidation. And he had sent Aziz to Geneva to make it clear that Iraq was ready to talk about a peaceful solution, but only after January 15. This was something that Secretary of State Baker would never accept.

Sitting in Aziz's suite while he was meeting with Baker were the Algerian Foreign Minister, Sid Ahmad Ghozali, and PLO Foreign Policy chief Farouk Kaddoumi. When the brief lunch break came after three hours of talks, Aziz walked into his suite and told Ghozali and Kaddoumi: "We're not going to make any progress in these talks. They will not discuss the 15th of January. They are not ready to lift the January 15 deadline. We can't negotiate with them unless they do."

There is one other important point to make about the meeting. During his press conference Aziz said that the Iraqi invasion of Kuwait had been linked with the Palestinian problem. That simply was not true. The invasion had originally been designed to solve the long-standing border issues between Iraq and Kuwait. It was only after Saddam Hussein discovered that this was not possible that he enlarged his objective to the Palestinian issue in his statement of August 12.

When Baker left Geneva the next morning to fly to Riyadh to meet with Saudi King Fahd, he told the press at the airport that he believed "the path to peace is open. The choice is that of the government of Iraq and I hope they will choose the path of peace."

For the world, despite other peace efforts being made, there appeared to be one last chance left. UN Secretary-General Pérez de Cuéllar was preparing to go to Baghdad to see Saddam Hussein. (But I had been in Amman in early September when Pérez de Cuéllar had met Tariq Aziz and that meeting had led to nothing.)

That night, January 10, Pérez de Cuéllar headed for Paris. He met French President François Mitterrand in the morning, then flew to Geneva for talks with the EC Foreign Ministers, whose request for a meeting with Tariq Aziz had been rejected. But if any one thought that Pérez de Cuéllar's meeting would result in peace, they had only to listen to what he said as he left Geneva for Baghdad: "I am going there in order to listen and be listened to by the Iraqi authorities . . . I have no proposals to make . . . Wish me luck."

What the world did not know was that Washington had already set the precise time for the start of the air war against Iraq: January 17, 2 A.M. Baghdad time.

Saddam Hussein had just learned that the U.S. Congress had voted the day before to support President Bush's plan for military action to free Kuwait. But he must have been confused by the message he was getting from the U.S. A large number of Senators and Congressmen had voted against the resolution, giving the impression that the United States was seriously divided on the Gulf issue. He did not understand the American mentality: once the war started, the American people would rally behind their President with little or no opposition.

When Pérez de Cuéllar arrived in Baghdad late in the evening of January 11 he had to wait almost forty-eight hours before he saw Saddam Hussein. He did have a meeting with Tariq Aziz, but night had fallen on Sunday, January 13, when he entered a room to meet the Iraqi President.

In early February 1991 the Iraqi government released what it said was the transcript of the meeting. Nobody has questioned the accuracy of the transcript. It is precise about the meeting, as were the transcripts of Saddam Hussein's meetings with U.S. Ambassador April Glaspie and U.S. chargé d'affaires Joe Wilson, which I obtained in Baghdad on my visit there in September 1990. It is important to understand what happened in Baghdad that night, only forty-eight hours before the January 15 deadline.

Pérez de Cuéllar opened the meeting by telling Saddam Hussein:

Mr. President, I should like to say that I have come to Iraq without being charged with any mandate; I am entrusted with no specific task, either by the Security Council or the United Nations. I have, however, been encouraged to make this trip not only by heads of state and governments but also by the Pope and by humble citizens who have asked me to take advantage of our position, particularly its moral aspect, to work for the establishment of peace in this region. It may surprise you, Mr. President, that among those who have wished success for my mission is the President of the United States, with whom I have met and talked four times since last Saturday. But I wish to assure you that I do not carry any message and I am no one's messenger. I represent only myself.

Before coming to Iraq, I met a week ago with President Bush and informed him of my decision to meet with you. I wanted, before doing so, to listen to him and to ascertain his wish with regard to finding a peaceful solution to the crisis. I cannot guarantee intentions, but all he said to me, knowing I was going to meet you, was that he desperately wanted a peaceful solution to the crisis.

You have taken certain initiatives, an important and constructive one of which was your decision to release the foreigners, by which you removed an obstacle in the way of the relaxation of the tension in the area. The August 12 initiative [in which Saddam Hussein had declared he was prepared to withdraw from Kuwait as part of a broader Arab solution, including the Israeli–Palestinian issue] has not been well understood, but it figures in one form or another in the first of the Security Council resolutions which specifically referred to the Arab League and its participation in any solution. On that basis something can be done. And you have done something, as I have told your Minister of Foreign Affairs. I consider that you have done a great deal for the question of Palestine; you have put the fate of the Palestinian people on your agenda. As a man of Hispanic origin, I feel I am close to the Arab world and to the Palestinian people.

Pérez de Cuéllar said that during his meeting in Geneva with the twelve EC Foreign Ministers on his way to Baghdad he had been told by the Ministers that they wanted to tackle the Palestinian problem.

Even Mr. Bush, when I saw him on Saturday, admitted the urgent need for tackling the crisis of Palestine and said that he has not forgotten the statement he made to the General Assembly on October 1, that perhaps there might be opportunities for all states to find a solution to the problem which has divided Arabs and Israelis.

But then Pérez de Cuéllar made the critical point that no other problems could be solved, including the Palestinian one, if Iraq did not withdraw from Kuwait.

I know your courage and generosity. I have followed the Iran–Iraq war and the initiatives you made from your side to end the war. I hope that in the same spirit you will offer something to put an end to the current dispute. Of course, to do so we must find a way of adhering to the United Nations resolutions, particulary 660 and 678 . . . There is something said by Mr. Bush which I put down on a small piece of paper. It is this: "The United States will not attack Iraq or its armed forces if withdrawal from Kuwait has been achieved and the situation has returned to what it was prior to August 2. The United States does not want to keep its ground forces in the region; it will support negotiations between the parties concerned, and I shall accept any decision taken by those parties."

When Pérez de Cuéllar ended, Saddam Hussein asked the UN Secretary-General, "Do you drink black coffee? This kind of coffee does not help one sleep at night."

Pérez de Cuéllar answered, "I travel too much. I am an old man but strong for my age. It is the head which controls everything."

Saddam agreed. "Yes, it is the head which regulates every-thing."

The Iraqi leader then started to outline his views.

I wanted you to come [he told the UN leader] because you know us and because you have dealt with us in the past and you know our pattern of thinking. But I was worried about your coming from a different angle because you are coming under conditions in which those who are capable of it are calling for the use of arms as quickly as possible. Therefore, when you cannot offer them what they want, they might find in your visit the pretext that they need to go to war. While listening to you, I can say that you have touched on several positive points. I agree with you that, with an issue of such complexity, solutions are not expected to be found in one meeting. These matters should be dis-cussed comprehensively and in depth.

For fifteen minutes the Iraqi leader went on to discuss the situation that had arisen during the Iran–Iraq war. He then turned to Kuwait.

What caused things to reach the point they have reached since August 2? It was the threat we felt. Kuwait had be-come a base in the hands of the United States to plot against us . . . We did not annex Kuwait or unite it with Iraq im-mediately, although you know that Kuwait's rulers fled on the first day, and that we brought it under control from the very first day . . . We agreed to the convening of a summit conference in Saudi Arabia, to be attended by five countries: Iraq, Yemen, Jordan, Saudi Arabia, and Egypt.

We wanted to discuss all these complexities with the Arab hemisphere and resolve them.

And what happened? Instead of convening the five-state conference, it was canceled by Saudi Arabia and Egypt, and they agreed with the United States to deploy its forces in Saudi territory. Thus we lost the opportunity for an Arab solution, and the Americans continued with deployment without a Security Council resolution.

Although the decision to deploy American forces in Saudi Arabia had already been made, we dealt constructively within Security Council Resolution 660. It is true that we have not recognzed the resolution. However, we dealt with its context. So we announced clearly that we would withdraw our forces on August 4. We did actually withdraw some of our forces. I think we pulled out one whole brigade, although the force we had there at that time was not as large as it is now. But when American escalation continued and U.S. forces continued to arrive in increasing numbers, we stopped the pullout of the force. As I have said, we declared the union and told the Iraqi people and army that Kuwait had become part of their country and they should fight for it to the death. [Saddam Hussein was referring to his announcement of August 8 that Iraq was annexing Kuwait.]

Saddam Hussein launched into the Palestine problem, criticizing the United States for opposing the convening of an international conference on the problem "so that it would not be scored as a political victory for Saddam Hussein . . . What are they saying now? Let Iraq withdraw from Kuwait, and then we will hold an international conference to discuss issues, and this is not a sure promise, but a mere possibility."

As the conversation went on it became clearer and clearer that Saddam Hussein was not ready to pull out of Kuwait without a larger solution. "The Iraqis will never withdraw in the face of death. Bush will therefore be pushed day by day into a corner, and he will be obliged to resort to arms because he who is busy preparing the requirements for the use of arms could not occupy his mind fully with thinking about how to find alternatives to avoid the use of arms," Saddam Hussein told Pérez de Cuéllar.

The closing exchange was vital. The UN Secretary-General put it clearly: "If I understood you correctly, your position on Kuwait is irreversible, and in this case we cannot operate according to the principle of the package."

"I did not say that," Saddam Hussein replied. "I have said what I have said. If you find out that the Americans are in the position of one seeking an outlet from a predicament and that they are searching for a way in which they will not lose but will not necessarily achieve all they want, it is possible to formulate guidelines for this purpose, and the Arabs could search for a solution in accordance with these guidelines."

Pérez de Cuéllar thanked Saddam Hussein for his hospitality and the time he had given him.

"I wish you success," Saddam said.

"We should think about our Palestinian brothers," said Pérez de Cuéllar.

"They are slaughtered daily—Palestinian children and women," the President replied.

Pérez de Cuéllar headed back to New York late in the morning of January 14, stopping in Paris to see President Mitterrand. He emerged from the meeting looking despondent. "Unfortunately, at the end of my trip I see no cause for optimism. I see no reason to have more hope than the day I left. I am a diplomat, but I am also honest and direct, and I cannot conceal that I made no progress in Baghdad."

There were no more than thirty-six hours until the January 15 deadline—midnight, Washington time. The French were talking about a last-minute peace effort and Foreign Minister Roland Dumas even indicated he was ready to go to Baghdad.

Then came January 15. In the early-morning hours the PLO leader Abu Iyad was murdered in Tunis. Dumas was still waiting to leave for Baghdad but said he would not go unless he got a message from Iraq that it was ready to withdraw from Kuwait. PLO leader Yasser Arafat was desperately calling leaders all over the Arab world, trying to move something in the direction of peace.

The deadline passed at midnight, and Iraq was still solidly stationed in Kuwait. Saddam Hussein was obviously waiting for war.

On the morning of January 16 I headed for my office early. I had the feeling that something was going to happen. At 4 P.M. the telephone rang. It was one of my top military sources, a man I completely trusted. "You better put your car in the garage tonight," he said and hung up. The message was clear. The attack on Iraq was coming that night.

At 11:30 P.M., London time, bombs started to fall on Baghdad. The Gulf War had started.

EPILOGUE

It was 12:30 in the morning of February 28 when my office phone rang next to the bed. I was told to come to the office immediately, as President Bush was going to make a statement to the American people at 2 A.M. For the fourth night in a row since the ground war had started, I roared out of bed, shaved and dressed rapidly, and headed for the office. When I arrived there were already bulletin documents on my desk indicating that he was going to announce the Gulf War was over. At 2 A.M. he announced the provisional cease-fire and the fact that air attacks against Iraq had been stopped and that the land war would end at midnight Washington time, 8 A.M. in Baghdad. The war had lasted six weeks and four hours, the crisis six months and twenty-six days.

I will leave it to military analysts to evaluate the war. It will take some time to break through the coded messages delivered to the press in Washington, Saudi Arabia, Israel, and Iraq to learn the details of what really happened. Some things were clear. The military capability of Iraq had been crushed. But the infrastructure of Iraq had also been destroyed, leaving a country that will take at least a generation to rebuild. Iraqi forces had also seriously devastated Kuwait. Important parts of Kuwait City had been destroyed, oil facilities set on fire, and citizens tortured and killed. But perhaps the most important impact of the war was the way it shook up and divided the Arab world.

The Arab nations are fragile, and each crisis in the region has resulted in dramatic changes. The creation of Israel in 1948 was seen as a massive Arab defeat. In the next five years the leaders of three countries, Egypt, Syria, and Iraq, were overthrown. During the Suez crisis, Iraq, then ruled by a royal family, allowed Britain to use its airports to attack Egypt with fighter aircraft. Two years later the Royal Family was ousted from power. The dramatic victory of Israel in the Six-Day war in 1967 led to the emergence of the Palestine Liberation Organization, at the height of its terrorist activity. And the 1982 Israeli invasion of Lebanon produced the hard-line, Iran-backed Hezbollah movement in Lebanon and, after five years, the Palestinian uprising in the Occupied Territories now known as *Intifada.*

In forty-five years since the end of the Second World War there have been eighty-one coup d'états in fourteen Arab countries, twenty-four of them successful. The two countries with the most coup d'états have been Iraq and Syria: thirty-two attempts, fourteen successes. The countries are monarchies and republics, but none of them is democratic. There are countries with "parliaments," "national assemblies" or "people's assemblies," but these are no more than phony structures created to provide the ruling élite with an aura of legitimacy. The failure of the Western powers who joined together in the Gulf War to press these countries toward democratic systems will add to the danger already created by the war. The failure of the Western powers to solve fundamental Arab problems like the Israeli–Palestinian conflict will add to that danger.

Experts have already issued lists of winners and losers in the Arab world. For them the winners are Iran, Turkey, Egypt, Syria, and Saudi Arabia. The losers are Jordan, Yemen, and the Palestine Liberation Organization. For the experts the winning personalities are President Ozal of Turkey, President Hosni Mubarak of Egypt, President Hafez el Assad of Syria, and King Fahd of Saudi Arabia. The losers are King Hussein of Jordan and Yasser Arafat of the PLO. But the fact of the matter is that those designated as winners have significant open or suppressed opposition in their countries, while King Hussein is highly popular in his and Yasser Arafat remains the dominant figure of the PLO. So no one should be surprised if some of the winners end up losing in the next few years and the losers maintain their popularity and power.

President George Bush has been talking about the creation of a new world order. But it will not be easy. American popularity has seriously dropped in some Arab countries. And U.S.–Soviet relations have become fragile, not long after the Cold War was declared to be over.

The European Community's push toward greater political and monetary union has been damaged by the war. And we should not forget that the war also created uprisings in many Asian nations.

It is difficult to argue against the American position that the war was a dramatic success. But peace is highly complicated, particularly in the Middle East. Defeating Iraq was rapid, but long-term peace may not be easy to achieve.

APPENDIX 1

Note from the Iraqi Minister of Foreign Affairs, Mr. Tariq Aziz, to the Secretary-General of the Arab League, July 15, 1990

Fraternal greetings.

I want to begin by recalling the principles in which Iraq believes and which it has always faithfully and conscientiously applied in its relations with the Arab world.

Iraq considers that the Arabs, over and above national boundaries, are one nation, that what belongs to them should belong to all and benefit all and that what hurts one of them hurts all. It is on this basis that Iraq has always considered the wealth of the Arab nation and has managed its own wealth.

Iraq also considers that, despite all that the Arab nation suffered during the Ottoman period, then under the yoke of Western colonialism, in terms of contempt, divisions, repression, and attempts to distort national identity, the components of its unity have remained solid and alive. Despite its division into states, the Arab world nevertheless remains one country, every inch of which must be considered in accordance with a nationalistic vision and, more particularly, in accordance with the demands of a common Arab national security. We must avoid falling into a narrow and selfish point of view when considering the interests and rights of this or that country. The higher interests of the Arab nation as well as the strategic calculations essential to Arab national security must be ever-present in our minds and must be paramount in inter-Arab relations.

It is on the basis of these loyal, sincere, and fraternal nationalistic sentiments that Iraq has established its relations with Kuwait, despite the past and present difficulties between Iraq and Kuwait, of which everyone is aware.

What motivated the present note is that we find ourselves, alas, faced with a situation that, because of the policy of the Kuwaiti government, not only completely contradicts the nationalistic principles we have just mentioned but threatens their very essence.

Although we have always insisted upon sincere fraternal relations and have always tried to pursue a dialogue with them at all times, the Kuwaiti leaders have undertaken, methodically and knowingly, to harm Iraq, attempting to weaken it at the very moment when it was emerging from a terrible eight-year war, during which, in the opinion of all sincere Arabs, leaders, intellectuals, and citizens, including the heads of the Gulf states, Iraq defended the sovereignty of the whole Arab nation, especially that of the countries in the Gulf and in particular that of Kuwait.

The Kuwaiti government pursued this deliberate policy of weakening Iraq at a time when the latter was faced with a savage Imperalist-Zionist plot because of her nationalistic position in the defense of Arab rights. Kuwait was, alas, driven by its egotism and its narrowness of vision but also by objectives that have shown themselves to be of the utmost seriousness and are described in the following pages.

1. As is well known, since the colonial era and the divisions it imposed on the Arab nation there has been an unresolved border dispute between Iraq and Kuwait, which the contacts established in the 1960s and 1970s did not succeed in settling and which still remained when the war between Iraq and Iran began.

During the long years of war, while the valiant sons of Iraq were shedding their precious blood at the front to defend Arab land, including that of Kuwait, and to safeguard Arab sovereignty and dignity, including those of Kuwait, the government of that country took advantage of the situation—exploiting Iraq's attachment to its genuine nationalistic principles and the nobility of its way of dealing with its relations with its brothers and with all Arab questions—to put a plan into operation, a careful and premeditated plan to eat away at Iraqi territory. Kuwait began to build military installations, an oil-producing infrastructure, and farms on Iraqi soil. At first we merely referred to these developments, thinking that that would be enough between brothers to make ourselves understood in the context of the fraternal principles to which we thought everybody subscribed. But the treachery continued unabated, which proves that it was carefully planned and premeditated.

After the liberation of Fao, we took the initiative—during the Algiers summit of 1988—of informing the Kuwaiti side of our sincere wish to settle this question in a friendly fashion in the context of the fraternal relations and higher interests of the Arab nation. The response was extremely surprising. It would have been logical for the Kuwaitis to greet our initiative with joy and to work toward a rapid settlement of the question. But what we saw on their side was deliberate hesitation and procrastination. All sorts of obstacles were created to hinder the continuation of the talks at the same time as the attack on our sovereignty continued with the construction of military, agricultural, and oil-producing installations on Iraqi soil.

Our patience in the face of these intrigues was due only to our wisdom and our honesty, and we could have borne even more, but things had taken such a serious turn that we could no longer remain silent. That will be the subject of our second point. We have kept records and can produce documents to prove all the excesses of the Kuwaiti goverment.

2. In the past few months—to be precise, since Iraq proclaimed the rights of the Palestinian people loud and clear and warned against the American presence in the Gulf—the Kuwaiti government has adopted an unjust policy whose object is to undermine the Arab nation and especially Iraq. Kuwait, with the complicity of the United Arab Emirates, has hatched a plot to inundate the oil market with a surplus far in excess of the quota allocated by OPEC. The pretexts it has used to justify this have been irrational, unjust, and without foundation and have not been shared by any other brother nation among the oil-producing countries. This policy has led to a dangerous collapse in the price of oil. After the fall experienced a few years ago in relation to the world averages, which then stood at $24, $29, and $28 a barrel, the attitude of the governments of Kuwait and the Emirates has caused a collapse in prices, making them drop from the already low minimum of $18 a barrel agreed to within OPEC to between $11 and $13. A simple mathematical calculation is enough to show the size of the losses suffered by the oil-producing Arab countries.

First, the average daily production of oil being 14 million

barrels, the collapse of prices experienced between 1981 and 1990 has lost the Arab countries about $500 billion, of which $89 billion were lost by Iraq. If the Arab countries had not lost such large sums, they could have devoted at least half to national development and aid to poor Arab countries.

By taking as a basis the minimum price fixed by OPEC in 1987—that is, $18 a barrel—the loss suffered by the Arab countries can be calculated as $25 billion because of the collapse in prices.

Second, every time the price of crude oil drops by $1 Iraq loses $1 billion over the whole year. The prices this year having dropped several dollars below the $18 fixed by OPEC because of the policy of Kuwait and the Emirates, Iraq has suffered a loss of earnings of several billion dollars at a time when its economy is in difficulty due to the military expenses incurred in the legitimate defense of its territory, its security, and its holy places, as well as the territories of the other Arabs, their territory, and their holy places, for eight long years. These considerable losses caused by the collapse in the price of crude have not been suffered only by the oil-producing countries. Their effects have also been felt in other friendly countries that benefited from the aid of those countries; the capabilities of the latter in terms of development aid have declined to the point at which some of them have been led to suspend it.

The situation of the specialized pan-Arab organizations has also deteriorated. They have been through grave crises and are now experiencing their most difficult time yet, as the subsidies from which they benefited have decreased or been suspended.

The Kuwaiti government has not been content with these attacks. It has launched others more specifically against Iraq. It has installed an oil-producing infrastructure in the southern part of the Iraqi field at Rumailah and has begun to extract oil from it. It therefore transpires that it has been inundating the world market with oil, of which part comes from the field at Rumailah. Iraq has thus suffered damage in two ways: its economy has been weakened at a time when it had most need of its resources, and then its wealth was despoiled. On the basis of prices between 1980 and 1990, the value of the oil extracted by Kuwait from the Rumailah field by this method, which is contrary to the rules of good neighborliness, is estimated at $2,400 million.

We affirm before the League of Arab States and before all Arab countries Iraq's right to recover the sums that have been stolen from it, as well as its right to demand reparations for the damage that has been done to it. Several times we spoke of the dangers of the policy being followed by Kuwait and the Emirates to the oil-producng countries, including Kuwait and the Emirates; we complained about it and put them on their guard. At the Baghdad summit President Saddam Hussein, frankly and in a fraternal spirit, brought up the matter with the Arab heads of state and in the presence of the parties concerned. (The text of His Excellency the President's speech is attached to this document.) We were convinced at that time that the governments of Kuwait and the Emirates were going to abandon that policy, especially as the climate of the Baghdad summit had been one of positive rapprochement. It has been painful to note that, in fact, all the bilateral moves and the contacts we established with our brother countries, so that they should intervene with the governments of Kuwait and the Emirates to convince them to abandon those methods, have been in vain and that, despite President Saddam Hussein's speech at the Baghdad summit, these two states have deliberately continued with the same policy. Some of their leaders have gone so far as to make arrogant statements when we talked about these truths and complained about them.

That is why we can only draw our own conclusions about the

intrigues of the governments of Kuwait and the Emirates. What we have here is premeditated policy with sinister aims, and it has become clear that this policy, which has led to a collapse in the price of crude, will finally undermine the economies of those countries themselves.

We can therefore not help but conclude that those who were so clear and so direct in their desire for this policy, those who sustained it and encouraged it, are merely carrying out part of the Imperialist-Zionist plan against Iraq and against the Arab nation, especially as the moment chosen for its implementation coincided with the threats uttered by Israel and the Imperialists against the Arab world and, in particular, Iraq. How, indeed, could we face this grave threat and conserve the balance of power we have managed to establish at the cost of all we suffered during the war when our principal source of revenue was experiencing such a collapse, as was that of all the oil-exporting Arab countries, that is, Saudi Arabia, Qatar, Oman, Yemen, Egypt, Syria, Algeria, and Libya? Add to that the disastrous consequences of this policy for the capacity of these countries to deal with the grave economic and social problems that for them are a matter of life and death.

What fate do the governments of Kuwait and the Emirates wish for the Arab nation in such difficult, delicate, and grave circumstances? In the service of what policy and for which objectives are they working?

Having explained the situation to all our brothers before, during, and after the Baghdad summit, having directly asked the two governments involved to put an end to this destructive policy because of the enormous damage it was causing, having sent envoys and letters, we condemn the action of the governments of Kuwait and the Emirates, considering it a direct act of aggression against Iraq and, clearly, against the whole Arab nation.

PIERRE SALINGER WITH ERIC LAURENT

The government of Kuwait has, indeed, committed a double aggression against Iraq: first by seizing part of its land and its oilfields and then by despoiling its national wealth. Such an act can be compared to an act of military aggression. Then deliberately trying to strangle the Iraqi economy at a time when Iraq is already subject to ruthless Imperialist-Zionist threats is also an act of aggression as serious as military aggression.

We are presenting the elements of this painful reality to our Arab brothers today in the hope that they will intervene to put an end to this blatant aggression, that they will make the offenders see reason and will advise them to resume the straight and narrow path and take into account the demands of our common national interest and our common national security.

3. Concerning the supreme interests of the Arab nation and the link between Arab wealth and the future of our nation, we put forward the following proposal: that all the Arab countries, oil producers or not, agree, on the basis of firm political solidarity, to raise the price of oil to $25 and then to establish an Arab aid and development fund along the lines of that suggested at the Amman summit. The fund would be financed on the basis of every extra dollar per barrel sold by the oil-producing countries over $15 and could bring in an annual sum of $5 billion. At the same time the oil-producing countries would see their revenues increase and would be able to protect themselves against any attempt to weaken the Arab nation through a decrease in its oil revenues.

Imagine what such a fixed sum could do to consolidate Arab national security and to ensure means of development for all the Arab states in the face of the grave economic crisis that most of us are experiencing.

Iraq submits this proposal for study in all seriousness. The next Arab summit in Cairo could be an opportunity to examine and adopt it.

4. Talking of these painful truths, it seems to us necessary to remove any doubts our brothers may still have concerning the aid provided to Iraq by Kuwait and the Emirates during the war.

All sincere Arabs agree that the war that Iraq had to wage was not merely in defense of her own sovereignty but also in defense of the eastern flank of the Arab world and of the whole Arab nation, especially the Gulf region. The Gulf leaders themselves admitted it openly.

The war was thus a common national struggle that Iraq took on in order to defend the security of our nation and the Gulf in particular.

During the war we received various kinds of aid from our brother countries in the Gulf, most of them in the form of interest-free loans. We received "aid" in this form at the beginning of the war, that is, up until 1982; after that we no longer discussed this aid, hoping that the war would not be a long one and that Iraq would immediately recover all her economic strength.

But the war continued, and its cost rose considerably. The military equipment purchased by Iraq alone cost $102 billion, paid in hard currency, not to mention the other military and civilian expenses that rose astronomically during the eight years of a savage war that extended over a front of 700 miles.

Although the aid given by our brother countries represented only a tiny proportion of what Iraq spent, in economic and in human terms, in the defense of the sovereignty and dignity of the Arab nation, the Iraqi leadership nevertheless expressed its profound gratitude to all the brothers who provided this aid. President Saddam Hussein publicly expressed this during visits made to Iraq by certain leaders of brother states in the Gulf.

However, the bitter truth, of which all Arabs should be aware, is that most of this aid was considered a debt that Iraq owed to the other countries, including Kuwait and the Emirates. We spoke of this, quite fraternally, to the interested parties a year ago, but they turned a deaf ear.

Moreover, Kuwait included as one of the debts owed to it the quantitites of Iraqi oil extracted from the Al-Khafji area and sold on Iraq's behalf after the closure of the pipeline across Syria, although these quantities had been sold as a surplus to Kuwait's OPEC quota. In order to present the full truth of this matter, we must explain an important aspect of the oil market during the war.

Before the war Iraq was one of the main oil producers, with about 2.6 million barrels a day. When war broke out production was suspended completely for several months, then began again on a small scale. The oil was exported through Turkey, then through Syria until 1982, when the pipeline was cut off. Iraq's oil exports in the south stopped altogether between 1980 and 1985, when the Saudi pipeline was opened. Iraq's losses during that period rose to $106 billion.

In point of fact, this sum had gone into the coffers of the other oil-producing countries of the region, which had increased their oil exports to compensate for the lack of Iraqi oil during eight years. A simple calculation is enough to show that Iraq's "debts" to Kuwait and the Emirates are easily compensated for by the surplus profits they made, thanks to their increase in oil production during the war.

The question we must ask is: since Iraq took on all the responsibility for defending the security and dignity of the Arab nation and for protecting the wealth of the countries in the Gulf—which would have fallen into foreign hands if Iraq had lost—must it still, despite everything, consider the aid it was given as a "debt"?

Didn't the United States give large amounts of taxpayers' money in aid to the Soviet Union and to its Western allies during the Second World War, although they were not part of the same nation? And after the war, through the Marshall Plan, America gave large sums for the reconstruction of Europe, acting in accordance with a global strategic vision of the interests and defense of the side to which it belonged and which had taken part in the war against a common enemy. How then can we continue to consider the amounts given to Iraq by brother Arabs as debts, when it contributed many times those amounts from its own treasury, and its youth gave its blood in defense of Arab land, dignity, and wealth?

Does not national logic and the logic of regional security compel us to follow the American example and force these countries not only to write off Iraq's debt but also to draw up an Arab plan, on the lines of the Marshall Plan, to compensate Iraq for some of the losses it suffered during the war?

This ought to be the logic of the Arab nation if only there existed a feeling of being part of Arabness and a desire for the security of the Arab nation. Instead of that, we see two of the governments in the Gulf—which Iraq protected by shedding the blood of its sons and even helped to enrich—now trying to destroy Iraq's economy by reducing its resources, and one of them, Kuwait, is even going so far as to steal the wealth of those who tried to protect its lands.

We present these bitter truths to the conscience of every sincere Arab, in particular to our brothers in Kuwait, so that they can measure the extent of our pain and the harm that has been done to us.

Tariq Aziz
Minister of Foreign Affairs of the Republic of Iraq
Baghdad
July 15, 1990

APPENDIX 2

Letter from the Iraqi Minister of Foreign Affairs to the Secretary-General of the United Nations, October 24, 1990

I am sending you a copy of a letter dated November 22, 1989, from the Director-General of the State Security Department to the Minister of the Interior of the former Kuwaiti regime. This dangerous document proves the existence of a conspiracy between that government and the government of the United States to destabilize the situation in Iraq.

I mentioned this conspiracy in a letter dated September 4, 1990, that I addressed to foreign ministers around the world. In that letter I explained the historical background and the machinations of the Kuwaiti leaders against Iraq as follows:

"We must therefore conclude that the leaders of the former regime wished to pursue their plots until Iraq's economy was destroyed and its political system destabilized. It is impossible to believe that a regime like that formerly in power in Kuwait could have embarked on such an ambitious conspiracy without the support and protection of a great power. That power can only be the United States."

I also made the following remarks in my letter:

"It is evident, from my historical account and from the description I have given of events, that the disagreement was not simply about economic or border questions. We had many differences of that nature over twenty years, and we always tried to maintain the best possible relations with the former leaders of Kuwait, in spite of their contemptible behavior and their despicable attitude toward Iraq. The fact of the matter is that there was an organized conspiracy, in which the former leaders of Kuwait deliberately took part with the support of the United States, to destabilize Iraq's economy and undermine its defense capabilities against the imperialist aims of Israel and acts of aggression on the part of the Arab world. To achieve that, it was necessary to undermine Iraq's political system and to strengthen the hegemony of the United States over the region, especially over its oil resources. In fact, as President Saddam Hussein declared at the Baghdad summit, and as I indicated in my letter to the Secretary-General of the Arab League, it was a war against Iraq."

This document proves, clearly and unequivocally, that the CIA and the intelligence services of the former government of Kuwait were in league with each other in plotting against the national security, territorial integrity, and national economy of Iraq.

I should be grateful if you would kindly circulate this letter and the appended text as official Security Council documents.

Tariq Aziz
Minister of Foreign Affairs of Iraq
Baghdad
October 24, 1990

APPENDIX 3

Letter from Brigadier Fahd Ahmed Al Fahd to His Excellency Sheikh Salem Al Sabah Al Salem Al Sabah

TOP SECRET AND PRIVATE

His Excellency Sheikh Salem Al Sabah Al Salem Al Sabah
Minister of the Interior

In accordance with Your Highness's orders, as given during our meeting with you on October 22, 1989, I visited the headquarters of the United States Central Intelligence Agency, together with Colonel Ishaq Abd Al Hadi Shaddad, Director of Investigations for the Governorate of Ahmadi, from November 12 to 18, 1989. The United States side emphasized that the visit should be top secret in order not to arouse sensibilities among our brothers in the Gulf Cooperation Council, Iran and Iraq.

I hereby inform Your Highness of the most important elements of what was agreed with Judge William Webster, Director of the United States Central Intelligence Agency, in the course of my private meeting with him on Tuesday, November 14, 1989.

1. The United States is undertaking to train individuals selected by us to protect His Highness the Emir and His Highness Sheikh Saad Al Abdulla Al Salem Al Sabah. The instruction and training is to take place at the headquarters of the United States Intelligence Agency itself, and we have set their number at 128, some of whom are to be used for special missions with the royal family, as determined by His Highness the Crown Prince.

In this connection the United States side informed us of its dissatisfaction with the performance of the Royal Guard forces at the time of the criminal attack on His Highness the Emir.

2. We agreed with the United States side that visits would be exchanged at all levels between the State Security Department and the Central Intelligence Agency, and that information would be exchanged about the armaments and social and political structures of Iran and Iraq.

3. We sought assistance from Agency experts in reviewing the structure of the State Security Department, which, according to the instructions given by His Highness the Emir, was to be accorded major priority at our meeting with the United States side. This would involve use of their expertise in drawing up a new strategy for action commensurate with the changes in the Gulf region and the country's internal situation, by developing a computer system and automating functions in the State Security Department.

4. The United States side said it was entirely willing to meet our request for an exchange of information concerning the activities of extremist Shia groups in the country and certain States of the Gulf Cooperation Council. Mr. Webster applauded our measures to combat movements backed by Iran and said that

the Agency was willing to take joint steps to eliminate points of tension in the Gulf region.

5. We agreed with the American side that it was important to take advantage of the deteriorating economic situation in Iraq in order to put pressure on that country's government to delineate our common border. The Central Intelligence Agency gave us its view of appropriate means of pressure, saying that broad cooperation should be initiated between us, on condition that such activities are coordinated at a high level.

6. The United States side is of the opinion that our relations with Iran should be conducted in such a way as, on the one hand, to avoid contact with that country and, on the other, to exert all possible economic pressure on it and to concentrate on effectively bolstering its alliance with Syria. The agreement with the United States side provides that Kuwait will avoid negative media statements about Iran and restrict its efforts to influencing that country at Arab meetings.

7. We agreed with the United States side that it was important to combat drugs in the country, after Central Intelligence Agency narcotics experts informed us that much Kuwaiti capital is being used to promote drug trafficking in Pakistan and Iran, and that the spread of such trafficking will have negative consequences for the future of Kuwait.

8. The United States side placed a special telephone at our disposal to promote the rapid exchange of views and information that do not require written communications. The number of the telephone, which is Mr. Webster's private line, is XXX.

I await Your Highness's instructions and convey to you my best regards.

(Signed) Brigadier Fahd Ahmed Al Fahd
Director-General of the State Security Department

FOR THE BEST IN PAPERBACKS, LOOK FOR THE

In every corner of the world, on every subject under the sun, Penguin represents quality and variety—the very best in publishing today.

For complete information about books available from Penguin—including Pelicans, Puffins, Peregrines, and Penguin Classics—and how to order them, write to us at the appropriate address below. Please note that for copyright reasons the selection of books varies from country to country.

In the United Kingdom: For a complete list of books available from Penguin in the U.K., please write to *Dept E.P., Penguin Books Ltd, Harmondsworth, Middlesex, UB7 0DA.*

In the United States: For a complete list of books available from Penguin in the U.S., please write to *Dept BA, Penguin*, Box 120, Bergenfield, New Jersey 07621-0120.

In Canada: For a complete list of books available from Penguin in Canada, please write to *Penguin Books Ltd, 2801 John Street, Markham, Ontario L3R 1B4.*

In Australia: For a complete list of books available from Penguin in Australia, please write to the *Marketing Department, Penguin Books Ltd, P.O. Box 257, Ringwood, Victoria 3134.*

In New Zealand: For a complete list of books available from Penguin in New Zealand, please write to the *Marketing Department, Penguin Books (NZ) Ltd, Private Bag, Takapuna, Auckland 9.*

In India: For a complete list of books available from Penguin, please write to *Penguin Overseas Ltd, 706 Eros Apartments, 56 Nehru Place, New Delhi, 110019.*

In Holland: For a complete list of books available from Penguin in Holland, please write to *Penguin Books Nederland B.V., Postbus 195, NL-1380AD Weesp, Netherlands.*

In Germany: For a complete list of books available from Penguin, please write to *Penguin Books Ltd, Friedrichstrasse 10-12, D-6000 Frankfurt Main 1, Federal Republic of Germany.*

In Spain: For a complete list of books available from Penguin in Spain, please write to *Longman, Penguin España, Calle San Nicolas 15, E-28013 Madrid, Spain.*

In Japan: For a complete list of books available from Penguin in Japan, please write to *Longman Penguin Japan Co Ltd, Yamaguchi Building, 2-12-9 Kanda Jimbocho, Chiyoda-Ku, Tokyo 101, Japan.*